Go To
DavidMeinz.com
to watch David's
Free Video

"HOW TO HAVE 100 HEALTHY BIRTHDAYS"

Published in St. Louis, Missouri, by Gilbert Press

Cover design and text composition by
Brinn Design, Summerville, SC

1st Edition
First printing, MMXV
ISBN 978-0-9644253-8-5

Wealthy, Healthy & Wise

How to make sure your money and your health last as long as you do.

David L. Meinz
MS, RD, FADA, CSP

"Wealthy, Healthy & Wise" is available for
quantity purchases at a significant discount.
Customized print runs for businesses
and organizations are also available.
For information, contact:

Gilbert Press, P.O. Box 70, St. Louis, MO 63042
1-314-838-5942

ENERGIZE!
Your Next Meeting With

DAVID MEINZ

David Meinz will show your people how to improve their personal and professional productivity.

A CONTENT RICH, FUN, AND FUNNY PROGRAM!
- The seven steps to increasing daily energy levels
- Surprising secrets about what you eat
- Living long and living well in the fast lane of life

TABLE OF CONTENTS

WEALTHY, HEALTHY & WISE

There are lots of books out there today that can help you plan for your financial future. Many promise to help you retire rich. You can tune in to a number of television and radio programs that offer what seems to be unlimited advice. Entire cable networks are dedicated to giving you the latest information on your stock portfolio.

Of course, having a sound financial plan is absolutely essential. The experts tell us to start saving from an early age, invest in long-term growth opportunities, and to be wise on how we spend what we make.

And yet, most financial experts overlook one important point. Even if you do everything right, you may end up with plenty of money but not be able to enjoy it. They fail to help you prepare in making sure your health lasts as long as your money does. Yes, I realize that's not their job. But surely the goal isn't simply to have enough money to pay all your medical expenses! Surely after all those years of work you should be able to relax, do what you want, and be *healthy* enough to enjoy it all.

As I've gone through life I've often found it ironic how many people strive for personal wealth, career success, and financial security only to totally ignore one of their most important possessions; their personal health. When it finally occurs to them later in life what their mixed-up priorities have cost them, they discover that their wealth can buy all the sick-care in the world, but not restore the health they so much desire.

That's why I wrote this book.

I created this guide to be used, not just read. Please don't just thumb through it and put it on a shelf. Nothing would make me happier than to someday meet you and see your copy marked-up, high-lighted, dog-eared, and flagged with post-it notes. And don't be fooled by the size of this book. It's jammed-packed with information you can use. I purposely made the dimensions small so it can fit into a man's suit coat pocket or woman' purse. I hope you take this book with you, especially when you travel or eat out. Here's what you'll find in *Wealthy, Healthy & Wise*:

■ SECTION 1: FISCAL FITNESS

For many of us, our fiscal fitness is just about as bad as our physical fitness. We're a nation of financial couch potatoes. When it comes to planning for the future, a lot of people are putting most of their hope into winning the lottery. Or living on social security. One's not likely, the other will simply keep you out of the poor house, but just barely. In this section we'll review some of the best time-tested advice for making sure you have enough money to not only meet your financial responsibilities during your working years but to have enough left over so you can actually enjoy the fruits of all those years of labor.

People are living longer, and are retired longer, than ever before. It's not that unusual for people to live well into their 80's and 90's, and beyond.

Believe it or not, the fastest growing sub-population group in the U.S. is the "Over 100" crowd! Many of these "centenarians" are actually still healthy and enjoying life. You will probably live longer than you expect; certainly longer in most cases than your parents generation.

Here's an important question: Will your money last as long as you do?

■ SECTION 2: ENERGIZE YOUR LIFE

In this section, I address the most critical aspects of what it takes to rev up your health and energy. For over twenty years now I've helped people increase their performance and productivity by improving their physical health. As an expert in the field, I have the advantage of knowing the scientific facts and latest research. But being a speaker, author, and entrepreneur means being on the road—a lot. I do some television and radio, too. I have to sleep in a lot of different beds, sit and autograph hundreds of books, and eat a lot of airport food. And early in my career, that routine started taking its toll – yes, even on me! I gained weight, my energy level dropped,

Yes, it is possible to balance being busy and productive with being healthy—once you know how. And it's often easier than you think.

and I realized that if I really wanted to be successful and stay in this business long-term, I needed to come up with some specific, realistic, usable, and flexible ways to maximize my health. I've put the lessons I've learned all together for your benefit in Section 2. And remember, you don't have to do everything all at once. You can start by picking a few strategies and add more along the way. Build on your successes.

Here's another important question: Will your health last as long as you do?

■ SECTION 3: EATING OUT

We love to eat out in this country! We spend almost half of the money we spend in our food budget on food consumed outside the home. For some people, it's even more. You need to spend that money wisely. Restaurant meals are notorious for being high in fat, salt, and calories. That's one reason that so many people are struggling with maintaining a healthy weight. Since it's such an important investment, both financially and from a health standpoint, I've dedicated the final section of *Wealthy, Healthy & Wise* to helping you make the right decisions when you go out to eat. People often ask me if it's ok to eat out. My reply is always "Well, yes and no." In this section you'll find lots of tips and

"Well, Yes and No" lists of menu choices at some 40 different restaurants. "YES" choices are either truly healthy or healthy compared to other available choices. "NO" items are generally meant to either show you the worst possible choices or alert you to the amount of fat and/or calories in a particular item. These lists aren't necessarily exhaustive; there may be other good and not-so-good choices that aren't listed here.

Making good choices is always easier once you know what the good and bad choices are. Making good choices when eating out works the same.

Nevertheless, the information that *is* here will take you a long way toward improving your health when you eat out.

Everything's related. You need money, but it's not of much value if you're sick. Yes, it's important to be healthy, but life isn't near as much fun if you're broke! It has always seemed clear to me that financial and physical health are closely related. I hope you'll strengthen *both* your financial and physical health through *Wealthy, Healthy & Wise*.

1

Fiscal
Fitness

**How to achieve prosperity
and financial freedom.**

TIMELESS TRUTHS

HOW TO MAKE A MILLION

If you could ask a thousand self-made millionaires how to become wealthy, you'd get a lot of great advice. However, you'd quickly learn that there are timeless truths to creating wealth that almost every financially successful individual follows:

- **THE FIRST PAYMENT:** They always pay themselves before meeting all their other obligations. When you sit down to pay your monthly bills, make the very first check you write one that you deposit into a savings account. Or, request your bank to transfer money from your checking to

The standard rule is to take 10% of what you earn and set it aside for saving and investing.

savings account automatically every month. If you're paid electronically, your employer may be able to make the savings deposit for you, which makes it even simpler.

- **DELAYED GRATIFICATION:** They all have the discipline of putting off a purchase that is not absolutely necessary. They remind themselves of their financial goals and keep their money focused on growing, rather than spending it.

- **COMPOUNDING:** They understand the power of compounding. They let their money multiply and increase their net worth 24 hours per day. They invest in things that grow in value rather than lose value; think IRAs not BMWs.

Experts say that it's a good idea to aim for having at least three months of your income socked away in an "emergency" fund for those unexpected expenses that come along.

RISK AWARENESS: They calculate their risk carefully. Many lower their risk by investing in a variety of things — so if one investment does poorly, the other investments balance the loss. And they buy insurance to protect themselves against catastrophic events.

MAKE MORE...SAVE MORE

- **GET** educated. College graduates can earn up to $1 million more than high school graduates over a lifetime.

- **THINK** stability. People who stay married accumulate more wealth than those who divorce. It costs less to maintain one household. Similarly, people employed with one company often build more wealth than "job hoppers."

- **LIVE** below your means. In the book "The Millionaire Next Door," millionaires profiled spent less than they earned and shopped for bargains. They were more concerned with financial independence than displaying high social status. Remember, wealthy people often save and invest 20% or more of their income.

- **DON'T** go into debt for things that don't build wealth (like restaurant meals, toys, etc.) and take a longtime to repay (such as vacations). That kind of debt can take years, even decades, to get rid of; by then the pleasure will be long forgotten and the cost of whatever you bought will be a lot higher than the original price thanks to all the added interest charges.

Remember to ask yourself: Is whatever you're buying worth creating debt?

AVOID THE CREDIT TRAP

- Plan ahead for a purchase. Save $25 a week for six months, and you'll have $650 for a new television.

- Establish your emergency fund of at least three months' expenses so you don't use a credit card for unexpected events such as car repairs.

- Use cash, checks, or debit cards. You can't spend money you don't have. (Unless you use a credit card!)

- Consider keeping credit cards at home instead of in your wallet.

Use credit cards for food, entertainment, clothing, and other disposable purchases only when you'll pay the bill in full every month.

- **BUY** products... not payments. If it's not possible for you to save for something and pay cash for it on the spot, always ask how many payments there will be to get it paid off. And remember to include any charges for interest.

For example, if there was no interest charged, you would pay $50 per month for five years to pay off an item that cost $3,000. With an annual interest rate of 9% you would be paying $62.28 per month, or a total of $3,736 by the end of five years.

Always ask yourself these four questions when buying anything:

1. *Do I really need this now?*

2. *How long would it take me to save up and buy it with no payments?*

3. *Can I get a good used one at a much lower price?*

4. *Is there something cheaper I can buy that would not require payments?*

■ **SAVE** on entertainment. Look for discounts at museums, zoos, and parks. Many offer free admission on certain days of the month. And don't forget about college campuses. They're a perfect source of great live performances at inexpensive prices.

If you don't already have a library card, get one. Not only can you save a lot by not buying books, but you can check out movies, TV episodes, and exercise videos for free or next to nothing. If you prefer to own, sites such as **www.titletrader.com** and **www.swap.com** can help you trade used books, movies, and music.

■ **KNOW** where your money goes. This may sound like a "no brainer" but not being aware of where your money goes can be a red flag that you are overspending. The "Tracking Your Expenses" worksheet at **www.smartaboutmoney.org** can help you monitor everything from utility bills to gifts and lunches. And that will help you find money to save too.

■ **TURN** $100's into $1000's by adding a little extra on your mortgage payments. If you ever needed a reason to send in a little extra with the house payment, take a look at what $100 can do. Say you have a 30-year, $200,000 mortgage at 6 percent interest. If you add $100 monthly you'll save over $49,000 and five years of payments!

If $100 is too steep, what about $50? To see how this would work for your circumstances, there are many free, online mortgage calculators. *When you send extra money, make sure*

Don't put off paying extra on your mortgage. Try to do it right from the beginning. If you wait, you'll have to increase the amount of "extra" to see the same savings.

to indicate that the additional funds are to be applied to the principal only.

HOW A LITTLE TURNS INTO A LOT

Socking away a little extra each week can have a big impact down the line. Here's what happens when you put aside just $20 a week:

- Saving $20 a week translates into more than $1,000 a year, plus interest.
- After 20 years at 5% interest, you'll end up with $36,100;
- After 30 years, it turns into $72,600.
- At 10% interest, the number grows to $65,500 after 20 years;
- After 30 years, it's a whopping $188,200.

INVEST wisely. Successful investors make regular deposits at regular time periods and hold high quality securities for the long term.

- **GET** tax smart. Wealthy people use legal ways to reduce income taxes including long-term capital gains, and tax-free and tax-deferred investments. But you don't have to be wealthy to use your taxes to keep more of your own money. Consider a consultation with a tax professional.

■ **RESIST** the idea of tax-refund loans. A refund anticipation loan is when a company gives you a loan in exchange for your tax refund when you get it. It may seem convenient when you need quick access to your refund. However, you need to be aware that this creates a situation where people can take advantage of you. Avoid businesses offering you refund loans that carry high fees and triple-digit interest rates.

Instead, file your returns electronically and ask that your refund be deposited electronically into your bank account. It may take as little as a week or two to get your refund this way.

■ **STAY** healthy. Chronic health problems like diabetes and obesity often are associated with less wealth. Reasons include medical expenses and reduced productivity. But remember, nothing yields a greater return on your investment than exercise.

Regular physical activity improves your quality of life and can reduce your risk for heart disease, cancer, stroke, diabetes, obesity, depression, arthritis, and other health problems.

Even if you don't start until middle age, you'll gain about two hours of life expectancy for every hour of exercise. That's about two years longer than your couch potato counterparts. But more importantly, the QUALITY of your last years of life will be much better. Exercise, eat nutritious meals, and quit smoking.

PLANNING FOR THE FUTURE

Whether you're close to retirement or it's still years away, you're probably concerned about financial security in later life. The good news is small steps you take today, and decisions you make as you get older, can greatly enhance your lifestyle.

Here's some tips to save enough money to live comfortably in the future:

DEVELOP A PLAN

Studies show that people who take time to crunch the numbers and come up with a retirement savings strategy save more money, on average, than those who do not. The American Savings Education Council's "Ballpark Estimate" is a simple six-step retirement planning tool. Calculations can be made online or by downloading a printed worksheet at **www.choosetosave.org**.

- **COUNT** on a long retirement. People are living longer and longer. That's a good thing. It means you have more time to enjoy life— and retirement. Retirements today often last 25 years or more and you'll want to have your money and your health last as long as you do.

SHOULD YOU SAVE FOR YOUR KIDS COLLEGE OR YOUR RETIREMENT?

Selfish as it may sound, if you can't do both, financial experts generally recommend that you save for retirement. Here's why:

- Other funding sources exist for college — such as loans and scholarships—but limited options exist for retirement.

- Without enough personal savings, retirees often must live on reduced income provided only by Social Security, or they have to continue working to make ends meet.

- Retirement savings are sometimes matched by an employer, but college savings are not.

- Students that are financially responsible for their education often are wiser consumers of their educational dollars.

■ **"FIND"** money to save. Consider refinancing your mortgage or reducing life insurance after children are grown. Keeping your car longer and saving money from expenses that end, such as child care and car payments, are other ways to free up money for savings.

■ **START** saving today. You can't earn interest on money you don't save. For every decade that you put off saving for retirement, the amount you'll need to save triples. A 35-year old must save $219 a month to accumulate $500,000 at age 65 while a 55-year old would need to save $2,421. Don't beat yourself up if you haven't been saving. Just get started today.

■ **CONSULT** a financial professional. If being a do-it-yourselfer isn't getting you to your financial goals, consider a relationship with a financial professional.

A professional can help you set realistic goals, develop a realistic plan to meet financial goals, put your plan into action, and help you stay on track. For many people, seeking professional help is "event-driven." Common events or needs that might motivate you to seek financial guidance include: rolling over your company retirement plan's lump sum, receiving an inheritance, preparing for marriage or divorce, planning for the birth or adoption of a child, caring for aging parents, planning for a special-needs child, or buying or selling a business.

IF YOU'RE PLANNING TO HIRE A FINANCIAL PLANNER:

- Hire someone with special credentials such as a Certified Financial Planner (CFP) or a Personal Financial Specialist (PFS).

- Ask what training and experience they have. Do they prefer to maximize earnings by taking more risk, or are they more conservative?

- Ask about their typical client. Will they provide you with references and the names of people who have invested with them for a long time?

- Understand how your planner is paid and be sure to find out how much it will cost to do business with them:
  - Fee-only (fees for providing advice),
  - Fee-based (commissions on some products they sell as well as fees you pay) or
  - Commission-based (paid by the companies whose products they sell).

- Check with state or federal securities regulators for any disciplinary problems or complaints.

- Be cautious of planners who handle one product — one family of mutual funds or one type of insurance. They may not be unbiased or able to give you comprehensive advice.

MAXIMIZE YOUR RETIREMENT SAVINGS

■ **MATCH** it: An employer's retirement savings account is a great way to build your nest egg. It's made even better if your employer happens to provide matches. This is "free money" that shouldn't be passed up. Many employers match up to a certain percent of their workers' pay. This means that, if you earn $40,000 and save 6% ($2,400), you'll save $1,200 more if you have a 50% match.

■ **MAKE** a 1% difference: When you get a raise, increase your retirement savings. Saving just 1% more of your pay can result in tens of thousands of dollars more at age 65. Here's an example. Let's say you're 40 and earn $40,000. You'd have an additional $41,080 at age 65 by saving an extra 1% of your pay annually and more than $60,000 with a 50% employer match.

■ **GO** for growth: Keep some of your retirement savings in stocks or growth mutual funds. These investments stand a better chance of staying ahead of inflation over time compared to bonds, CDs, and money-market funds. Never invest in anything that you don't understand or feel comfortable with, however.

- **CONSIDER** delaying retirement. By waiting just three years to retire, you could stretch your retirement savings another seven to 10 years. How? Three important reasons:

  - *Compound interest on savings that you're not withdrawing.*

  - *Higher pension and/or Social Security payments.*

  - *Continued earnings and savings. Plus you'll continue to receive employer benefits.*

- **THINK** about working during retirement. Many people want to work after they retire. Sometimes it's due to financial need, but often it's because they find working enjoyable. Besides income, work provides social contacts and a sense of purpose. There are also the financial benefits of not having to tap into your retirement savings.

- **STRETCH** your savings withdrawals. Withdraw money from taxable accounts first. Leave tax-deferred accounts growing as long as possible. If you can, try to let them grow until the mandatory withdrawal age of 70 ½. If you change jobs, try to put the retirement account money you've earned from your previous employer in an IRA-rollover account to keep your savings tax-deferred. Another money-stretching strategy may be converting a traditional IRA balance to a Roth IRA. Check with a financial expert to see if this makes sense for you.

MAKE A LITTLE EXTRA MONEY

Like to work with wood or sew? Have an interest in photography? If you have a hobby that you enjoy and think others would appreciate what you make or have to offer, consider turning your interest into a side business you can do in your free time. A sideline business can provide money to save now and may give you a little job that you can continue into retirement.

PROTECTING YOUR PLAN

You've insured your home, your car, and your life. What about your ability to work? How much of your savings would be gone if you couldn't earn an income for an extended period of time?

The fact is that three in 10 workers entering today's work force will become disabled before retirement. And disabilities cause half of all home foreclosures and are a leading cause of bankruptcy.

Disability insurance helps pay your bills if you can't

work because of illness or injury. Short-term insurance pays benefits after a wait of up to 14 days, but the benefits last no longer than two years. Long-term benefits may take several months to begin, but last longer. Most plans end coverage at age 65, so you may want to cancel your policy when you get close to retirement.

If you buy coverage through your employer with pre-tax dollars, any benefits you receive are taxable. If you pay for private insurance with after-tax dollars, the benefits are tax-free.

Here are some points to consider when shopping for disability insurance:

- *Compare both the price and the definition of disability.*

- *Buy a non-cancelable policy, if possible. It's renewable with no premium increase. With a guaranteed renewable policy, the premiums may go up.*

- *Buy when you're young. The cost rises as you age.*

- *A longer waiting period lowers your cost.*

- *A residual benefit allows you to work part time and receive partial disability payments.*

- *Cost of living adjustments increase your benefits as the cost of living goes up. You pay more for this.*

AVOID MAKING THESE TOP LIFE INSURANCE MISTAKES

- **NO INSURANCE:** Almost a third of U.S. households have no life insurance — a mistake if you have dependents relying on your income.

- **NOT KEEPING UP:** Review your policy periodically. For example, if you have children or receive large raises, you may require additional coverage.

- **GENERALIZING COVERAGE:** Beware of one-size-fits-all "5 to 10 times your annual salary" formulas to determine the amount of life insurance. Be sure to ask for a personalized analysis based on your circumstances (such as the age and number of children and spouse's income).

- **INSURING MINOR CHILDREN:** Children are typically dependents so there's generally no reason to insure them unless they contribute significantly to family income.

- **ACCIDENTAL DEATH RIDERS:** Whether you die in an accident or while asleep shouldn't affect the amount of insurance you buy. These riders are expensive and coverage is limited. If your family needs twice as much insurance to live comfortably, buy a larger policy.

- **RISKY LIFESTYLE:** Life insurance premiums are risk-based. You can pay more (or be denied coverage) if you have poor health habits (such as smoking and obesity), a poor driving record, or dangerous hobbies.

PREPARING FOR LIFE CHANGES

BEFORE YOU TIE THE KNOT

It's a fact, money problems are the number one reason marriages fail. Whether you're getting married for the first time or remarrying, these questions can help you focus on how you'll manage money. Have each partner write down answers separately and then discuss the responses:

1. What financial assets are you bringing to this marriage?

2. What are your regular income sources?

3. What are your current and potential liabilities? Include credit card debt, mortgages, alimony, child support, promises to pay for college or care for aging parents, etc.

4. What type of health, life, auto, and disability insurance coverage do you have?

5. How much money do you like to have in savings to feel comfortable?

6. What is your income tax liability? A single work-

ing parent who takes the "head of household" deduction may increase the amount of tax owed when they file a joint return as a married person.

7. Do you have anything extraordinary in your financial history or credit report, such as a personal or business bankruptcy?

8. How much retirement income will you have? Has any of it already been committed to a former spouse?

9. How do you want to handle day-to-day finances? Will you want a joint checking account or separate accounts? Who will pay monthly bills?

The conversation may be a little uncomfortable but it can save a lot of future heartache (and money!) Do it before you walk down the aisle.

AS YOUR PARENTS BEGIN AGING

Some of the issues that come with aging parents can be difficult—for both sides. But those things need to be discussed. It's important that your parents understand that there may come a time when they'll need some help.

These tips may help you ease into the conversation without making your parents feel that you're greedy or trying to take over:

- **GET** their advice. Say something like "I'm putting my will together. How did you go about doing this?"

- **TALK** about a recent news story that focuses on topics such as seniors who can't afford prescription drugs or who have large amounts of debt.

- **HELP** your parents look for ways to cut costs, such as finding a less expensive phone service, utility company discounts, or health fairs that offer free diagnostic screenings. Ask questions like: "Have you thought about how you will pay for heating costs this winter?"

- **OFFER** to take a financial planning workshop with your parents. Free or affordable programs may be available through your state or county cooperative extension service.

- **ASK** your parents where you can find their information on bank accounts, insurance policies, and other important documents in case of an emergency.

Very often, adult children help with the care of elderly parents, especially if they're nearby and the goal is to keep the parents in their home. The hidden, but very real, cost for those adult children is the impact on work. Many caregivers take a leave of absence from work or quit working entirely.

THE COST OF CARE

If your aging parents need help, there are numerous options, from in-home "homemaker services" to assisted living facilities. Here's how the costs compare. All are national median rates.

- Licensed homemaker services: $18/hour
- Licensed home health aide services: $19/hour
- Adult day health care: $60/day
- Assisted living facility (one bedroom, single occupancy): $3,185/month
- Nursing home (private room, skilled nursing care 24 hours a day): $206/day

BECOMING SINGLE AGAIN

If you're recently widowed or divorced, most experts will advise you to postpone major financial decisions until you heal emotionally. In the meantime, these steps can help you move toward financial stability:

1. Put enough money to cover your estimated expenses for the next six to 12 months in an

Inces..

easily accessible account. If you're divorcing, open an account and credit card in your own name. If your spouse has died, keep funds from savings in a safe account until you are ready to make long-term investments.

2. Organize your financial documents to begin planning for future expenses. Gather information from bank statements, credit card bills, retirement and pension plans, tax returns, and other financial records.

3. If you're a widow or widower, check with an attorney about how to probate your deceased spouse's will. You may need to go to court to be named as the executor to begin carrying out your spouse's wishes.

4. Request several copies of the death certificate so you'll have it to send to banks, Social Security, life insurance companies, etc.

DON'T LET ANYONE PRESSURE YOU INTO MAKING LONG-TERM INVESTMENTS

Take a family member or trusted friend with you to meetings with financial advisers and attorneys. They can take notes and help you follow up with action plans.

YOUR HEALTH AND FINANCES

CUTTING HEALTH CARE COSTS

- **FOCUS** on prevention. Good health habits can reduce the risk of costly medical problems. Examples include: recommended screening exams, eating nutritious food, exercise, washing your hands frequently, and flossing your teeth.

- **NEGOTIATE** a discount. If you're responsible for all or part of a medical bill, request a price break for paying cash. Cash payments save the doctor or hospital the processing fee on credit cards. Ask about a discount for prompt payment. If you can't pay promptly, ask about a payment plan.

- **FOLLOW** the rules. Read the "fine print" in your health insurance policy regarding referrals to specialists and pre-certification for medical procedures. Not knowing the rules can result in denial of coverage for a claim.

- **GET** with the program. Look for free or low-cost health fairs, well-child clinics, flu shots, gyms, and other local health-related services available.

WHAT YOU SHOULD KNOW ABOUT GENERIC PRESCRIPTION DRUGS

With prescription drugs, a higher price doesn't necessarily mean it's a better product.

- A generic drug is chemically identical to its brand-name counterpart, but typically costs much less.

- Consumers save $8 to $10 billion dollars a year when they purchase generic drugs. The average brand-name prescription costs $198, while the average generic costs just over $72.

- Many health insurance plans pay a greater percentage of the cost of a generic drug than a non-generic drug. The average co-payment for a generic drug is $6. The average co-payment for a brand-name drug is $29.

- About 75% of all brand-name drugs have a generic equivalent. As top-selling brand-name drugs lose their patent, more and more generics will become available.

- You can find out if a medication has a generic and how much you could save if you switched to a generic version by linking onto the Food and Drug Administration's "Electronic Orange Book" at **www.fda.gov/cder/ob**, visiting **www.drx.com**, or asking your pharmacist.

- Most doctors are receptive to patients who ask for generics. If a generic is not available, an alternative medication in the same class of drugs may be available in generic form.

- **USE** mail-order prescriptions. If possible, order a 90-day supply by mail instead of getting a 30-day supply from a local pharmacy. The savings are generally 15% to 35% on monthly co-payments.

- **BE WARY** of investing in any over-the-counter "anti-aging" products. Remember that marketers are not required to prove their effectiveness and they are not regulated by the U.S. Food and Drug Administration. Americans spend more than $20 billion every year on anti-aging remedies like cellulite creams and dietary supplements like human growth hormone (HGH). Nonprescription HGH that is taken as a supplement and not given as a shot degrades and becomes useless before it reaches the bloodstream.

IS HEALTHY FOOD TOO EXPENSIVE?

While processed foods may look cheaper, they can actually end up costing you a lot more over time in poor health. Fortunately, there's a lot of things you can do to lower food costs without sacrificing nutrition:

- **TRY** main-course meals that use less meat and more vegetables, such as tacos, a stir-fry with a small amount of chicken or beef, or stews and soups packed with vegetables and legumes.

■ **MAKE** food from scratch. It's worth the time. Prepackaged foods are usually higher in fat, calories, sodium, sugar, and price. Bring home-made snacks when the family goes out so you won't be tempted to stop for fast foods.

■ **FIND** a balance between regular and organic foods. Organic tends to be more expensive, but if you do want to buy at least some organic fruits and vegetables, choose those that collect the most chemicals when conventional growing methods are used. These include: apples, bell peppers, celery, cherries, hot peppers, imported grapes, nectarines, peaches, pears, potatoes, red raspberries, strawberries, and spinach.

Consider the cost per serving when you buy fresh produce. If you're paying by the pound, you'll be paying for the weight of inedible seeds and rinds, too.

■ **DON'T** pay for water. When buying fresh greens by weight, shake them well before you put them in the grocery bag. Leaves can store a lot of excess water and weight.

■ **READ** nutrition labels when you compare different brands of the same product.

PLANNING MEANS SAVING

Take fewer trips to the grocery store. If you make three trips a week and spend just $10 each trip on impulse buys, that can amount to $120 extra each month. By planning ahead and shopping only once a week you'll probably spend only $40 per month on impulse purchases. That saves you $960 a year!

- Plan your meals a week in advance and make a shopping list.

- Don't shop when you're even a *little* hungry.

- Check for items on sale. Use a store's website, smartphone app, or weekly flier when making your list.

- Don't assume all coupons will save you money. Even with a coupon, a more popular brand item may be still be higher than that of a lesser known or generic brand. And be honest about whether it's a good idea to buy three boxes of double fudge cookies just because it's a "good deal."

- Visit these websites for big potential savings on groceries: **www.TheGroceryGame.com**, **www.SavingsAngel.com**, and **www.Alice.com**

- Shop at discount food outlets, and stores that sell generic foods, their own brands, and foods in bulk. But always be sure to check the expiration dates on milk and other perishable foods. Foods on sale may be starting to get old.

CHECK the unit price on foods; it's usually in small print on the shelf. You may be surprised to find that buying a larger container does not always save you much.

■ **BE AWARE** that special dietetic or diabetic foods are more costly and usually not necessary.

■ **SUBSTITUTE AND SAVE:**

- Boneless cuts of meat may be a better buy — since you're not paying for the bone.

- White eggs have the same nutritional value as brown eggs — which are more expensive.

- Buy plain frozen vegetables instead of those packed in butter or other sauces.

- Regular or quick-cooking oats are less expensive than instant oats.

■ **DO-IT-YOURSELF SAVERS:**

- Make your own small bags of snacks instead of paying the high cost for small single-serving bags.

- Buy a large container of nonfat yogurt and separate it into single servings.

- Make your own cooking spray by putting vegetable oil in a spray bottle.

- Use nonfat powdered milk for cooking and baking.

THINK GLOBAL, BUY LOCAL

The trend toward local foods is booming. Buying local benefits you and your community, and can benefit the environment by reducing the energy and waste it takes to transport, store, and package non-local foods. And nothing beats the flavor of "picked at peak" fresh produce. Here's some ideas on buying local:

- Farmers Markets: Many farmers offer a discount on "imperfect" items they may have, so be sure to ask. To find a market close to you visit **www.ams.usda.gov/farmersmarket**.

- On-Site Farm Stands and Pick-Your-Own: Ask about discounts on larger quantities of already picked produce and share the savings with family or friends. And pick-you-own can especially be cost effective for those who like to can or freeze. Classifieds are a great source to find seasonal availability and locations.

- CSA Memberships: Community Supported Agriculture is a way to buy seasonal foods (typically produce) direct from local farmers. Members purchase "shares" before the growing season and in return receive a weekly "share" of that seasons' crops. For more information and to find a CSA near you visit **www.localharvest.org/csa**.

DON'T BUY AN EXPENSIVE CLOTHES RACK!

Before you invest a lot of money in home exercise equipment, there are a few things you should do.

Are you already committed to getting at least 30 minutes of exercise every day? You may think buying a machine will motivate you to get in shape, but it usually doesn't work that way for most people.

Start by buying inexpensive things like dumb-bells, exercise bands, a stability ball, or an exercise video. If you regularly use these things, then consider more expensive items.

■ Avoid purchasing sight unseen. Visit different gyms and stores to "test drive" and compare products. Look for machines that will allow you to work harder as you become fit. Equipment should be easy to learn and adjust to various body sizes if more than one person will be using it. In general, don't buy fitness equipment from TV infomercials.

■ Make sure you have enough room. If the only place you can put it is in your garage, will you really use it during the cold winter and hot summer months?

- Think about your goals. Treadmills, stationary bicycles, rowing machines, and stair climbers will give you a good cardiovascular workout, build endurance, and help you lose weight. Free weights and multi-station machines (sometimes called home gyms) build strength. Stability balls are good for balance and flexibility.

WHAT ELSE COULD YOU BUY WITH THAT CIGARETTE MONEY?

It's hard to kick the habit. But thinking about how much money you'll save and what else you could buy with that money just might make it easier. How many tanks of gasoline could you buy, for instance, if you gave up smoking?

PACKS VERSUS GALLONS		
PACKS PER DAY	COST PER YEAR*	GAS IT COULD BUY*
1 Pack	$2007.50	501 gallons
2 Packs	$4015.00	1003 gallons
3 Packs	$6022.50	1505 gallons
Based on $5.50 per pack of cigarettes and $4.00 per gallon of gas.		

When you quit smoking, the savings start to pile up right away. If a one-pack-a-day smoker quit and put the $2,007.50 in an investment account in equal monthly payments earning 5% compounded interest every year for 25 years (age 40 to 65, for example), they would end up with right at $100,000! Wouldn't that be a nice retirement bonus?

STAYING HEALTHY WHEN TIMES ARE TOUGH

Everyone knows poor health can create financial stress. But we hear less about the impact of financial stress on health.

Financial stressors such as job insecurity, job loss, and home foreclosure can increase the body's level of stress hormones. Over time these stress hormones can have a significant impact on your health. They may raise the risk of heart disease as well as contribute to anxiety, depression, and reduced immunity.

To help reduce the impact of financial stress:

- Exercise to lift your mood and sharpen your focus for creating solutions. (See *Move Your Body* on page 55.)

- Don't cut yourself off from other people. Seek out the social support of friends and family.

- Get 8 hours of sleep every night. This is especially critical during highly stressful times when the body and brain need added rest and repair.

- If you're feeling blue or down, get help from your doctor or a mental health professional.

- Eat a healthy diet. Many people look to food for comfort during difficult times but end up actually feeling worse in the long run.

Try to eat lots of fruits and vegetables, and avoid high sugar and fatty foods, especially those that are high in trans fats and saturated fats like fatty meats or French fries.

Be sure to read the next section, *Energize Your Life,* for much more on how to feel your best no matter what your circumstances.

2

Energize
Your Life

How to put more years in your life
and life in your years.

FEED YOUR BRAIN

Studies show that your brain chemistry is affected by what kind of food you eat, when you eat it, and how much of it you eat. That brain chemistry affects focus, concentration, problem solving, mood, and how you feel in general. It helps your brain work at its maximum potential too. And it's that brain that controls everything you do.

HEART SMART IS BRAIN SMART

Your brain needs the proper amounts of oxygen and blood to run at peak performance. That's where a "heart healthy" diet comes in. By helping

Whenever you see one of those little heart symbols or the words "heart healthy" next to a menu item, consider it brain food.

your heart and arteries to function well, it also helps your brain to function well.

In several studies, the Mediterranean diet–which includes fish, whole grains, moderate amounts of red wine, olive oil, and nuts–has been shown to result in lower rates of Alzheimer's disease and depression. And research is showing that the omega-3 fats found in fish, also considered heart healthy, may also help brain function, as well.

THE POWER OF PROTEIN

There's good reason to include protein in your meals, especially at breakfast and lunch. A meal that emphasizes protein, like a grilled chicken breast, causes an increase in the brain neurotransmitters *dopamine* and *norephinepherine* which can make you feel more energized and alert. That's exactly what you want. On the other hand, a meal higher in carbohydrates causes an increase in the production of *serotonin* which helps you feel more relaxed and calm. A higher carbohydrate meal, like pasta, is perfect toward the end of a long and stressful day.

But when it comes to protein, make sure to choose a lean source. Many proteins also come with excessive fat and a meal that's high in fat takes longer to digest and can slow you down.

HERE'S A FEW CONVENIENT AND EFFECTIVE HIGHER-PROTEIN SOURCES:

- **EGGS:** one whole egg has about 6g. of protein; one egg white has 4g. of protein; 1/4 cup egg substitute has 6g. If you have high LDL cholesterol, limit yourself to no more than four egg yolks a week or use egg whites or egg substitutes which have no fat or cholesterol.

- **JERKY:** on average, 1oz. has around 11g. of protein and only about 1g. of fat. Unfortunately they're usually very high in salt. As an alternative check out "Ostrim." It's one of the few with reasonable sodium. GNC usually carries it or visit www.protos-inc.com.

- **COTTAGE CHEESE:** one cup has a whopping 32g. of protein! Again, sodium is high. I use the 1% "Friendship" brand with only 120mg. of sodium per cup. If you mix in a bit of fruit you won't miss the salt.

- **YOGURT:** one cup of has about 12g. of protein. "Greek" yogurt can have as much as 24g. Choose low fat and leave some of the "fruit" in the bottom of the container; it's mostly sugar.

- **MILK:** one cup has 8g. of protein. Drink skim or 1%, you don't need the extra saturated fat in 2% and whole milk.

- **TUNA:** one 5oz. can has about 25g. of protein. I eat chunk light. That way I don't have to worry about the higher levels of mercury associated with albacore and yellow fin tuna.

CARBS ARE GOOD FOR YOU

Despite what fad diets come and go, *the fact is that your energy comes from blood glucose and that comes from the carbohydrates you eat.* But choose carbs closer to the way they grow. Whole grain breads and cereals, not white; whole fruits and vegetables, not their juices. These complex carbohydrates take longer to digest than simple carbohydrates that tend to be more processed. As a result, they're better at keeping your blood sugar (glucose) levels stable. That means you'll feel better and have more consistent, sustained energy.

You Should Know: 4 grams of sugar on a food label equals 1 teaspoon of sugar

High sugar foods, and other simple carbohydrates, dump a lot of sugar into your blood quickly and give you a short-term energy spike. But it doesn't last. That spike causes your body to release insulin to try to bring your blood sugar levels back down, often resulting in them being lower than before you ate.

EAT BREAKFAST

Mom was right on this one. Unfortunately, only about one third of American adults eat breakfast.

RESEARCH SHOWS THAT PEOPLE WHO EAT BREAKFAST:

- Weigh less, on average, than those who skip it

- Give their metabolism a jump start

- Have an easier time losing and maintaining weight

- Are less likely to develop type 2 diabetes or heart failure

- Are better nourished overall

- Show signs of enhanced memory

- Benefit from increased attention span & ability to think

(And generally tend to be a little less grumpy!)

If you're not already one of them, start tomorrow. Try to eat as early as you can—ideally within the first hour of waking up. Remember, your brain runs on glucose, which is depleted overnight while you sleep. If you're not hungry at breakfast, start with a *little* something. You can work up to more over time.

The best breakfast includes whole grain complex carbohydrates, protein, and a small amount of fat to help slow the release of glucose into the blood. Try to get as close to that as you can. A breakfast like pancakes with syrup or a Cinnabon puts you in the mood to relax and take it easy, not get started with the day's work. You can do better than a bear claw from Dunkin Donuts.

GIVE THESE A TRY:

- A bowl of slow cooked or instant oatmeal (or other whole grain cereal) made with milk instead of water, and some raisins and nuts

- French toast made with whole-grain bread instead of white, topped with vanilla yogurt and maybe a little cinnamon. (honest, it's very good)

- Smoked salmon on a whole-wheat bagel with a slice of tomato and low fat cream cheese

- Whole grain bread with peanut butter and a glass of milk

- Granola with yogurt and fruit

- A smoothie using frozen berries and bananas, skim or almond milk or yogurt, honey and peanut butter

Check out the Eating Out section for some good breakfast choices when you go out to eat.

When it comes to breakfast don't limit yourself to conventional thinking. You don't have to eat "breakfast" foods at breakfast. There's nothing wrong with a bowl of cereal at night and a turkey sandwich in the morning.

EAT LESS, MORE OFTEN

Try this: Eat breakfast, have a small snack around mid-morning, then lunch, followed by a mid-afternoon snack and, finally, dinner. Just spread out the same number of calories you're eating now. Schedule your snacks by paying attention to when you tend to get hungry and plan to eat a little something about a half-hour before that.

Fruit, string cheese, nuts, and whole-grains crackers will give more sustained energy and nutrition than an energy drink. Here's some more ideas:

- Peanut butter and apple or other fruit, yogurt with berries, hummus and baby carrots
- A smoothie made with frozen fruit, milk, and protein powder.
- Mixed dried fruit and nuts, one half ounce each

Smaller amounts of food are easier to digest than large meals and aren't as likely to cause your blood sugar to spike. Be patient though, it may take a little while for you to get used to eating like this. By the way, eating smaller meals, more often, is one of the top strategies people cite for successful weight loss and maintenance.

WHATEVER YOU DO, DON'T SKIP MEALS.
It usually leads to fatigue and overeating at the next meal.

WATCH OUT FOR ENERGY & PROTEIN BARS

- Consumerlab.com tested 30 popular bars and found that most underreported the fat, salt and calorie content.

- A "high energy" label *does not* mean it will increase mental alertness. Legally, that simply means it's high in calories.

- A good guideline for nutrition and sports bars is to make sure they contain at least 8 g of protein, and no more than 3 g of saturated fat, 13 g of sugar, and about 200 calories.

- Not all fiber is created equal. The fiber that's added to energy bars is often not as good as what you get from whole foods.

- If your bar has more than 100% of any particular nutrient don't eat more than one of them in a day. Too much of certain vitamins and minerals can be a bad thing.

- Look for ingredients that are whole grain, like rolled oats. Remember that things like *brown rice syrup* or *high fructose corn syrup* are just sweeteners.

EAT CLOSER TO THE WAY FOOD GROWS

One of the reasons people feel fatigued is that they don't consume enough *quality* food. In human studies, the better your nutritional status, the better your mood, ability to think, and memory. The nutritional quality of food often decreases as processing and refining increases. You're better off with an apple instead of apple juice; brown rice instead of white rice; a chicken breast instead of chicken nuggets. Ask yourself, does a Twinkie grow that way??

Try to eat a total of 4 ½ cups of fruits and vegetables per day. It may sound like a lot, but one banana quickly does away with about one cup of that. And eat the whole fruit or vegetable, don't just drink their juices. Go to www.myplate.gov for more on how much of each food group you need.

MOVE YOUR BODY

If you want more energy, start burning more energy. That doesn't make sense but people who exercise regularly will tell you it's true. Aerobic exercise increases your metabolism, elevates your mood, and can help you sleep better too. It doesn't take much. One study found that fatigued adults boosted their energy levels by an average of 20% just by participating in light or moderate cycling three times a week for about 20 minutes per session.

Please don't kid yourself. You will never *find* time to exercise. Those that are successful at integrating fitness into their lifestyle report that they *schedule* exercise. Putting an activity session into my appointment book has done more to integrate fitness into my life than all the good intentions in the world.

Besides regular exercise, even a brisk 5-minute walk makes for a quick pick-me-up.

Here's the FIT formula:

- **FREQUENCY:** Exercise three to five times a week. If you're trying to just maintain your fitness level, three times. If you're trying to improve it and take fat off your body, five.

- **INTENSITY:** We're starting to de-emphasize the Target Heart Rate formula. It turns out it doesn't apply to a lot of people. Instead, just get your heart pumping faster, and build up a sweat.

- **TIME:** Experts now recommend 150 minutes of moderate exercise, like brisk walking, a week or 75 minutes per week at a more intense level for exercises like jogging. That's per WEEK, not per day. Come on, you can find 75 minutes a week!

Be sure to also include some type of weight resistive exercise at least twice a week. And stretch after, not before, your workout. You'll get more benefit when your muscles are warmer. You'll also have better sustained energy if you eat a little something light 30-60 minutes before you begin and after you finish your workout.

FITTING IN FITNESS AWAY FROM HOME

There's actually a lot of ways to get in some exercise while traveling. You should be able to maintain your fitness level if you can get two to three exercise sessions in per week. Try to complete any exercise more than two hours before bedtime; later than that can make it harder to fall asleep.

■ Be sure to pack a pair of walking shoes. If you have a long layover at the airport, put your roll-on bag in a locker and take a walk. You can also pack a jump rope or exercise DVD to play on your laptop in the hotel room.

■ One of the simplest, best exercises is to climb stairs. Not just one flight though. If it's safe and you feel comfortable, the stairwell at your hotel can give you an incredible workout. It burns more calories than walking or jogging, plus strengthens the glutes and leg muscles too.

■ Of course, most hotels now have some basic fitness facilities available. If they have a swimming pool consider some invigorating laps to begin or end your business day. You can also ask your local health club if they're a member of the IHRSA Passport Program. It allows you member privileges at thousands of health clubs around the United States, Canada, and abroad.

THE SHORT WALK THAT COULD SAVE YOUR LIFE

To avoid blood clots, also known as Deep Vein Thrombosis, take a walk around the airplane cabin every hour or two.

Since dehydration can cause your blood to get thick, be sure to drink plenty of fluid.

If you're at increased risk for blood clots because you have high blood pressure, are overweight, take birth control pills, or have a tendency for your legs to swell, consider taking a 325 mg aspirin the day before your flight and on the day of travel. Ask your doctor.

LOSE BODY FAT

Notice I didn't tell you to lose "weight." Since muscle weighs more than fat, if you lose fat and gain muscle, which is the goal, the bathroom scale may not move as much as you had hoped. Even when you're eating healthy, exercising, and feeling good, the scale can make you feel like you've failed. Research shows that losing body fat boosts energy and mood. Stay focused on that.

Don't go for the quick weight loss that most diet books promote either. There's a difference between quick, temporary weight loss and long-term, successful body fat loss. Weight loss that comes off quickly is usually regained quickly as well.

The three steps to successful body fat loss are:

- **ONE:** Eat less calories, primarily by decreasing sugar and fat. Gram for gram fat has over twice the calories of protein, carbohydrates, and even sugar.

- **TWO:** Make regular physical activity part of your lifestyle.

- **THREE:** Stop worshipping the bathroom scale. It doesn't tell you the whole story. Buy a tape measure instead. By the way, fat around your mid-section is a lot more dangerous than hip fat.

And remember, prevention is the best medicine. You never have to exercise fat off your body if you never put it on in the first place.

DRINK UP

Being dehydrated can make you feel tired. After all, your brain is made up of 75% water. So even a little dehydration can significantly affect your energy level and bring on fatigue and headaches. And yes, contrary to what you may have heard, beverages other than water *do* count towards your fluid requirements, including coffee and alcohol. But, ideally, water is what your body wants.

DRINK MORE WATER

Water contains no sugar, caffeine, or artificial chemicals. Your body *likes* water. So drink around eight, eight-ounce cups throughout the day. Your system needs plenty of fluids for optimal performance. Your energy level will suffer without them.

And remember, the air on a commercial airplane is very dry. That loss of body water can contribute to jet lag and can increase the danger of blood clots when flying. Be sure to drink plenty of fluids.

COFFEE IS OK

Surprise! Coffee isn't bad for you. At least if you keep it to about three 8-10 oz. cups or less a day. Moderate amounts of caffeine don't appear to have

When you order coffee, always add you own sweetener. Some places add up to 9 teaspoons of sugar in a large coffee. Even YOU wouldn't add that much!

any significant health risks. However, those with heart palpitations, irregular heartbeat, anxiety, or high blood pressure would do well to decrease their caffeine intake. If you do decide to cut out coffee, do it slowly to minimize the withdrawal symptoms.

Of course, if you're sensitive to caffeine, try not to drink any after about 3 p.m. That will let the effects wear off by the time you're ready for bed. If you're a regular or heavy coffee drinker, understand that the morning boost you get is actually the coffee counteracting caffeine withdrawal. A true energy boost from coffee is only experienced by those who don't use it on a regular basis. I'm not against coffee, it has its benefits, but it should never be your primary source of energy. A cup of coffee does NOT count as breakfast.

DRINK FOR HEALTH

Moderate alcohol consumption seems to decrease heart disease risk. That's two drinks a day for a man or one drink a day for a woman. Women with a family or personal history of breast cancer should

ONE DRINK EQUALS

12 oz = 1.5 oz = 5 oz

not drink at all. Try not to drink alcohol after 6 p.m. Even though alcohol is a depressant and can make you drowsy, its effect on your sleep cycle can cause you to wake up in the middle of the night, and makes the sleep you do get less restful. That won't help your energy levels.

PASS ON THE ENERGY DRINKS

Unlike most other beverages, energy drinks are considered a supplement and are therefore unregulated by the government. While the FDA limits caffeine content in soda to 71 mg. per 12oz. can, energy drinks can have two or three times that amount, sometimes in a much smaller container. Some do use artificial sweeteners, but many are loaded with sugar as well. In addition, they usually contain the amino acid *taurine, guarana* (another form of caffeine), and a whole list of other additives we really don't know enough about to determine side effects or any dangers from long-term use.

Reports of negative reactions, and even deaths due to over or improper use, have prompted several countries to actually ban some energy drinks. And several major-league baseball teams have now restricted their use after finding they can contribute to dehydration.

As far as the B vitamins in some energy drinks, they do help convert carbohydrates–like sugar–into energy. But having 2000% of the recommended daily allowance is overkill. B vitamins are water soluble, meaning that what the body doesn't need gets urinated out. By the way, most Americans get plenty of B vitamins already. Deficiencies are quite rare.

Bottom line, energy drinks are okay for most people when used occasionally. The problem is many people don't use them just occasionally. If you need a boost in energy, an unsweetened cup of coffee may be a better choice. It will have no sugar, around 100 mg. of caffeine, and only about 2 calories.

AN IMPORTANT WARNING

Don't ever mix an energy drink with alcohol. Mixing a stimulant, caffeine, with a depressant, alcohol, seems to decrease coordination, alertness, and response times even more than alcohol with just a regular mixer. *Even worse, people who drink these concoctions feel more awake and alert and are more likely to drive when they shouldn't.*

IMPROVE YOUR IMMUNITY

Being sick is bad enough. But being sick with the flu or a miserable cold that goes on for days and days is almost unbearable. Taking steps to improve your immune function is well worth your time and attention.

So what exactly is immunity? It's the network of cells and organs, like your tonsils, spleen, and lymph nodes that work together to help protect you from disease. Unfortunately as you get older, the immune response doesn't work as efficiently, making prevention even more important. What's more, those over 50, or with chronic illness, are more susceptible to complications from being sick.

WORTH A POUND OF CURE

Here's what we know helps improve your immune function, and decrease your chances of getting the flu and/or colds:

- **MINIMIZE** your exposure to viruses. You've heard it before, but it's important: wash your hands frequently with soap, and keep them away from your nose and eyes. By the way, washing your hands should take about 60 seconds. That's 2-3 times longer than most people take.

Hands that are slightly wet are more likely to transfer bacteria and viruses to and from the next surface you touch. Always dry them well after washing.

EAT nutritious food. A nutritional deficiency can negatively affect your immune system. So be sure to hit your goal of 4½ cups total of fruits and vegetables every day.

▪ **ENGAGE** in moderate exercise. Studies found that women who walked briskly for about a half hour five days a week had about half the sick days as their sedentary counterparts. When they did get sick, their illnesses were milder. Interestingly, very intensive exercise doesn't seem to help. Studies show that after a marathon, participants are *more* susceptible to infections.

▪ **FIND** ways to combat stress. Those under stress are more likely to develop colds, are slower to heal from wounds, and are less responsive to vaccines than are people experiencing less stress. On the other hand, successfully dealing with stress, and practicing stress management techniques actually improves immune function.

■ **LIMIT** the amount of fat in your diet. Not only will this help you control your calories, but a study at Tufts University found those with a lower than average dietary fat intake had better T-cell function, a measure of immunity. A diet lower in simple sugars may also help.

■ **DECREASE** your daily calories. Slightly decreasing the calories of an otherwise nutritious diet is the only intervention ever proven to work to increase healthy lifespan in laboratory animals. It probably works in humans, too. This slight decrease, along with losing a few extra pounds, seems to increase immune function by, once again, increasing the activity of T-cell function.

■ **GET** enough sleep. One study found that those who averaged less than seven hours of sleep a night were three times more likely to catch a cold than those who averaged eight.

■ **MAINTAIN** a positive outlook. The research shows that those who express a more positive, upbeat personality are much less likely to develop colds when exposed to cold viruses.

- **GET** your flu shot. Flu viruses change from year to year so get it annually. And do it in October or November so the vaccine can get to its full effectiveness as the flu season matures.

- **STAY** current on other vaccines. Ask your doctor about immunizations that can protect you against pneumonia, tetanus, hepatitis, cervical cancer, and shingles. It's now recommended that adults over 50 get the shingles shot. The shot can be expensive but talk to someone who's had shingles. Once you have it, you'd pay almost any amount to be cured. If there was a cure. All you can do is get the shot to help prevent it.

YES, YOU CAN FIGHT A VIRUS

We now have antiviral drugs that can stop the flu in its tracks. Even once you have it. But you have to act fast for them to work.

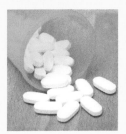

Since travel exposes me to so many germs, my physician has given me a supply of an antiviral drug I take at the very first sign of a problem. Ask your physician what's best for you.

GO TO BED

If you want to operate at peak performance, there's no room for compromise in this area. Your body is VERY sensitive to a sleep deficit. *Even missing one hour can affect you for the next several days.* Lack of sleep can make you irritable and impair your motor skills. It can decrease your ability to think, to make decisions, and to be creative. It can also lead to increased stress hormones, increased blood pressure, weight gain, an increased risk of cardiovascular disease, and a weakened immune system. Maybe you should just go ahead and skip Leno and Letterman.

Experts suggest that most people do best on 8 1/4 hours per night. The *average* American gets about seven, meaning there are those out there trying to get by on even less. It seems that among some in the corporate world, not getting enough sleep means you've "arrived" and is almost a badge of honor. Don't buy into it. Doing so comes with an increased risk of colon cancer, strokes, diabetes, heart attacks, and early death.

> *For every 100 people who claim they only need about five or six hours of sleep, only about 5 actually do.*

KEYS TO A GOOD NIGHT'S SLEEP

- Stop drinking caffeinated beverages too late in the day. Keep in mind that it takes about five or so hours for the effects of caffeine to wear off.

- Don't take a hot bath immediately before going to bed. Although it's relaxing and seems like it should help you get to sleep, it actually can make it harder. Your body needs to cool to a certain temperature to maximize your ability to sleep.

- The National Sleep Foundation says 90% of us stay up late to watch TV. The bedroom should be used for two things. Sleep is one of them. TV is not the other. Move the television out of your bedroom, start using TiVo, and get to sleep!

- Go to bed and get up at about the same time every day. Even on weekends. Your energy levels will be better if you sleep and rise on a regular routine.

- Get it quiet, cool, and dark. Keep the room temperature on the cool side; between 65° and 72° F. Dim the alarm clock light and use pull-down window shades.

- Avoid melatonin. It doesn't come in standardized doses and we don't know what dosages are effective or if long-term use is safe. It may help promote sleep in some people, but if taken at the wrong time it can make the situation worse.

- Aim your diet more toward carbohydrates in the evening, it will increase levels of the calming brain neurotransmitter, serotonin.

A LOT OF GOOD THINGS HAPPEN WHILE YOU SLEEP

- Getting enough sleep improves both memory and learning. Research shows that while you're asleep, your brain actually restores information that was lost during the day, stabilizing and protecting memory.

- Sleep seems to improve physical performance as well. It can also help reduce stress levels and that, in turn, can help control blood pressure.

- A recent study found that C-Reactive Protein, which measures inflammation in the body, was higher in those who got six or less hours of sleep per night. Inflammation is related to most every disease and chronic health issue we know of.

TAKE A NAP

Thomas Edison did it. Winston Churchill did it. Ronald Reagan did it. They still got a lot done.

A short nap can boost your mental energy and performance. However, if you sleep too long it  *can make you groggy and may interfere with your ability to fall asleep at night. Keep it to about 30 minutes or so.*

A recent report in the *Annals of Internal Medicine* found that overweight people lost more body fat and retained more lean muscle when they slept about eight hours versus five hours a night. Other studies have found an increase in calorie intake and abdominal fat as sleep goes down.

■ Sleep helps improve emotional stability, so if you find yourself moody or depressed, getting adequate sleep may help.

3

Eating Out

How to stay healthy when someone
else does the cooking.

NOTE: Restaurants and other food establishments constantly change their menu offerings and recipes. The nutritional values listed here are accurate and up-to-date as of the time of book publication.

MUST-KNOW BASICS

Going out to eat used to be a "once in a while" splurge. But now, the average American gets more than a third of his daily calories from food consumed outside the home.

Compared to a home-cooked meal, the average restaurant meal is usually 20% fattier; higher in calories, sugar, salt, and cholesterol; lower in calcium, fiber, and iron; and large enough for two adults—averaging 1000 calories. Fortunately, there's a lot you can do to offset the potential downside.

THE POWER OF ASKING

Don't be afraid to ask for what you want. Be politely assertive. Many restaurants will prepare your request—even if it's not on the official menu. That way you're the one who controls what you eat.

BE SURE TO ASK FOR:

- A doggie bag to be delivered with your meal and put half away before you start eating.

- Dressings, sauces, and toppings on the side.

- Mustard instead of mayo; broccoli rather than cole slaw; a baked potato in place of fries; and salsa, not butter or sour cream for the potato.

AND ASK IF:

- There are side orders of vegetables or fruit available—they usually are.

- Sharing a meal is allowed.

- You can order from the senior menu, the portions are smaller.

- Lunch size portions are available for dinner.

IMPORTANT SODIUM WARNING

The sodium values in restaurant food are consistently, unacceptably high.

To avoid discouraging you from choosing otherwise healthy options, sodium values have been left off the menu listings in this section. If your physician has told you to limit your sodium, you also need to limit how often you eat out. On days that you do eat out, minimize salt for the rest of the day. Increasing your intake of foods high in potassium will also help.

POTASSIUM RICH FOODS

While sodium can raise blood pressure, potassium can help counter-balance that effect. So eat plenty of potassium rich foods every day. Aim for a daily intake of at least 4,700 milligrams.

TRY THESE:

POTASSIUM
(in milligrams)

Baked Potato, medium w/skin	925
Spinach, 1 cup cooked	800
Avacado, 1 cup cubed	730
Prune Juice, 1 cup	710
Halibut or Yellowfin Tuna, 4oz cooked	600
White Beans, 1/2 cup canned	595
Yogurt, 8oz plain	580
Baked Sweet Potato, medium w/skin	540
Orange Juice, 1 cup	500
Brussels Sprouts, 1 cup	495
Winter Squash, 1 cup	495
Lima Beans, 1/2 cup cooked from dry	480
Broccoli, 1 cup cooked	460
Cantaloupe, 1 cup cubed	430
Tomatoes, fresh, 1 cup chopped	430
Banana, medium	420
Carrots, 1 cup chopped	410
Apricots, dried, 1/4 cup	380
Milk, nonfat , 1 cup	380

Some medications will affect your potassium levels, ask your doctor.

ALERT: Similarly named items can vary greatly in calories and fat from one restaurant to another. ALWAYS ask how food is prepared and order appropriately using the suggestions in this guide.

WHAT TO LOOK FOR:

- Any foods whose description indicates that they are lower in fat: *grilled, broiled (not in butter), flame cooked, steamed, poached, roasted, baked, cooked in its own juice.*

- Any fish not deep-fried or swimming in butter. Salmon is one of the best choices you can make on most menus, and though it's higher in fat than most fish, it's the good omega-3 variety. If you can, choose wild over farmed salmon. *But be sure to use cocktail sauce, not tartar sauce or butter on seafood.*

- The healthier menus and menu items many restaurant chains now offer. And look for the heart healthy symbols next to selections.

...AND WHAT TO LOOK OUT FOR:

- The hidden fat terms used in menu names or descriptions: *breaded, flaky, puffed, crispy, batter-dipped, tempura, creamy, scalloped, buttery, hollandaise, béarnaise, and au gratin.*

FORGET the "diet plate" or typical chef salad with about 900 calories and 70 fat grams. You can easily do better.

An iceberg lettuce salad is not much more than water with dressing. Choose salads with dark greens like spinach and romaine lettuce for better nutrition.

HEALTHY CHEESECAKE?

The Cheesecake Factory now offers a healthier menu. With about 40 items under 590 cal., their "SkinnyLicious" menu has plenty to choose from.

- SkinnyLicious Tuscan Chicken is about 800 cal. less than their Teriyaki Chicken.

- At under 590 cal. SkinnyLicious Turkey Burger, beats the 1370 cal. regular version.

BEFORE GOING OUT TO EAT...

- See if the restaurant's menu is online. If so, you can narrow your choices without feeling pressured to make a quick decision. And use their nutritional analysis if it's available.

- Check out *www.HealthyDiningFinder.com* to find healthy choices at restaurants when you're at home or on the road.

LIQUID CALORIES ARE NOT EQUAL

It's much easier to overconsume calories from drinking than eating:

- Research shows that liquid calories don't signal the body's "satiety center" like calories that come from solid food. Eating 200 calories of pasta is going to satisfy you a lot more than drinking 200 calories of soda.

HAVE A HAPPY ENDING

FOR DESSERT look for sorbets or the mini desserts many restaurants now offer. Dessert Shooters—dessert in a shot glass—are usually 100-300 calories. One regular dessert with three or four forks is a good idea too.

Applebees™ Blue Ribbon Brownie has 78g total fat, 40g saturated fat, and a whopping 1670 calories.

HOW MUCH IS A SERVING?

PASTA: One cup of plain cooked pasta is about the size of a tennis ball and averages 190 cal. A typical restaurant portion is 3-4 cups!

RICE: One cup of plain rice is also about the size of a tennis ball, has around 220 cal. and under 1g fat; brown rice is just a little more.

BAKED POTATO: A medium size, plain potato is around 150 cal. Most places serve a large, which averages about 260. But the bohemoths at some places are over 600 cal., and that's with nothing on it!

MEAT: Three ounces of meat, poultry or fish is considered one serving, and looks like a deck of playing cards. Most restaurants put at least twice that on your plate.

FAST FOOD

On a typical day, Americans order 200 hamburgers per second. And we're eating more fast food than ever. In 1970, we spent about $6 billion on fast food; in 2000, more than $110 billion! The choices at fast food restaurants are getting worse–and better–at the same time. Today's fast foods usually contain way too much salt, fat, and cholesterol, or they can actually be a part of a nutritious diet. It all depends on what you choose when you get there.

FRIES WITH THAT?

- *The average small order of fries is usually about 340 calories and 15 grams of total fat. Don't forget to add that to your meal's overall fat and calorie content.*

- *A Wendy's plain baked potato topped with a small order of chili is a great alternative, loaded with nutrition and fiber, too. It tastes great, it's a complete meal in itself, and only has 480 calories and 6 grams of total fat.*

EAT FAST AND EAT WELL

Here's a few examples of how different choices can make a real difference. Big or small, they all add up to better health.

	Total Calories	Total Fat (g)	Saturated Fat (g)
CHICK-FIL-A Grilled Chicken Sandwich	320	5	1.5
INSTEAD OF:			
BURGER KING TenderGrill Chicken Sandwich	410	16	2.5
ARBY'S Roast Beef Classic Sandwich	360	14	5
INSTEAD OF:			
ARBY'S Roast Turkey & Swiss Sandwich	700	28	7
KFC mashed potatoes & gravy	120	4	1
INSTEAD OF:			
KFC potato salad	210	11	3
TACO BELL Fresco Crunchy Tacos, 2	300	16	5
INSTEAD OF:			
TACO BELL Fiesta Beef Taco Salad	780	42	10
McDONALD'S Newman's Own Low-Fat Italian Dressing, 1.5oz.	50	2.5	.5
INSTEAD OF:			
McDONALD'S Newman's Own Ranch Dressing, 1.5oz.	170	15	2.5

WELL, YES AND NO

RESTAURANT	Total Calories	Total Fat (g)	Saturated Fat (g)
Arby's YES!			
Jr. Roast Beef Sandwich	210	8	2.5
Roast Beef Classic Sandwich	360	14	5
Beef & Cheddar Classic Sandwich	450	20	6
French Dip & Swiss/Au Jus	450	17	8
Jr. Chicken Sandwich	310	17	2.5
Original Mighty Minis, Roast Turkey, 2	330	7	1.5
Chicken Biscuit	370	17	11
Prime-Cut Chicken Tenders, 3	350	17	2.5
Arby's Sauce *(Tangy BBQ, 30cal. more)*	15	0	0
Horsey Sauce	50	5	.5
Chopped Farmhouse Roast Turkey Salad, no dressing *(w/lite italian add 20cal./1g. fat)*	230	13	7
Chopped Side Salad, no dressing	70	5	3
Balsamic Vinaigrette Dressing	130	12	2
Jr. Chocolate/Jamocha/Vanilla Shakes *approx.*	350	9	6
Arby's NO!			
Sausage, Egg & Cheese Croissant	550	42	17
Chicken Bacon & Swiss-Crispy	600	29	7
Reuben Sandwich	640	30	8
Roast Turkey & Swiss Sandwich	700	28	7
Buttermilk Ranch Dressing	210	22	3.5
Au Bon Pain YES!			
Asiago Cheese Bagel	370	8	4.5
Cinnamon Raisin Bagel	320	1	0

cont'd next page

WELL, YES AND NO

RESTAURANT Au Bon Pain YES! (cont'd)	Total Calories	Total Fat (g)	Saturated Fat (g)
Honey 9 Grain Bagel *(Sesame/Poppy is similar)*	310	2	0
Plain *or* Onion Dill Bagel	280	1	0
Plain *or* Wheat Skinny Bagel	90	1	0
Low-Fat Triple Berry Muffin	290	3	.5
Warm Apple Bake	80	3	2
Plain Croissant	280	5	9
2 Eggs on a Bagel	430	12	4
Smok. Salmon & Wasabi w/Onion Dill Bagel	410	10	4.5
Egg Whites & Cheddar Breakfast Sandwich	250	9	6
Apple Cinnamon Oatmeal, sml	230	3	0
Strawberry Passion Fresh Fruit Smoothie	190	0	0
Greek Van. Yogurt & Wild Blueberry Parfait	340	6	1
Brie, Cheddar, Fruit & Crackers	310	19	10
Butternut Squash & Apple Soup, 16oz.	280	10	3.5
12 Veggies Soup, 16oz.	240	8	.5
Black Bean Soup, 16oz.	360	2	0
Chicken & Vegetable Stew, med.	340	19	5
Chicken, Chickpea & Tomato Salad (Petit)	200	9	1
Caprese Sandwich, 1/2	310	14	6
Classic Chicken Salad Sandwich	450	12	2
Grilled Chicken Sandwich	480	15	2
Black Angus Roast Beef & Herb Cheese Sandwich, 1/2	260	7	2.5
Turkey & Swiss on Farmhouse Roll, 1/2	320	11	5

WELL, YES AND NO

RESTAURANT Au Bon Pain YES! (cont'd)	Total Calories	Total Fat (g)	Saturated Fat (g)
Tuna Salad Sandwich	470	14	2.5
Chicken Caesar Asiago Salad	250	10	4
Thai Peanut Chicken Salad, no dressing	190	5	1
Tuna Garden Salad, no dressing	270	12	2
Salad Dressing: Balsamic Vinaigrette, 2oz.	110	9	1.5
Fat Free Raspberry Vinaigrette, 2oz.	110	0	0
Light Ranch Dressing, 2oz.	120	11	2
Soups, sml (8oz.) *at or under* Carrot Ginger, Chicken Noodle, French Onion, Garden Vegetable, Cabbage, Kale Tomato Florentine, Vegetable Beef Barley *Most others are under 200cal./10g. fat,* *except bisques or those with cream or cheese.*	100 or less	4 or less	2 or less
Chicken and Vegetable Stew, sml	220	13	3
Mayan Chick. Harvest (brn)Rice Bowl, entree	580	17	4
Chocolate & Creme Torsade	230	9	6
Brownie Bites	160	7	2
Chewy Marshmallow Bar	250	5	3
Gingerbread Cookie	210	4.5	.5
Au Bon Pain NO!			
Almond Croissant	500	31	13
Double Chocolate Chunk Muffin	580	25	7
Carrot Walnut Muffin	540	25	5
Veggie & Hummus Wrap	670	38	9
Newport Turkey Sandwich	770	34	14

cont'd next page

WELL, YES AND NO

RESTAURANT Au Bon Pain NO! (cont'd)	Total Calories	Total Fat (g)	Saturated Fat (g)
Caprese Sandwich, whole	550	27	13
Broccoli Cheddar Soup, (16oz)	450	32	15
Bleu Cheese Dressing, 2oz	310	33	6
Pecan Roll, 6oz. *(Crumb Cake is similar)*	740	43	18
Boston Market YES!			
"Meals Under 550 Calories" as served w/sides			
Rotisserie Chicken, 1/4, white	320	13	4
Rotisserie Chicken, 1/4, white, no skin	220	2.5	1
Rotisserie Chicken, 3 pc, dark, no skin	280	12	3.5
Turkey Breast, lrg	280	12	0
Macaroni & Cheese (kids)	330	13	8
Garlicky Lemon Spinach	110	9	5
Steamed Vegetables *(Green Beans are similar)*	60	2	0
Mashed Potatoes, *(w/2oz. gravy, add 20cal.)*	240	10	5
Cinnamon Apples	250	3.5	.5
Rotisserie Chicken Carver Sandwich, 1/2	375	17	4
Roasted Turkey Carver Sandwich, 1/2	425	23	4.5
Caesar Salad, 1/2, w/dressing	220	14.5	3
Chicken Noodle Soup, 14oz.	270	8	2.5
Boston Market NO!			
Meatloaf, lrg *(even reg size still has 30g. fat!)*	760	44	19
Rotisserie Chicken Pot Pie	820	48	23
All White Rotisserie Chick.Salad Sand., whole	890	56	9
Creamed Spinach, side	250	20	12

WELL, YES AND NO

RESTAURANT	Total Calories	Total Fat (g)	Saturated Fat (g)
Burger King YES!			
Egg & Cheese Croissan'wich	330	18	8
Maple Flavor Quaker Oatmeal	170	3	1.5
BK Veggie Burger, no mayo	390	16	2.5
Hamburger	230	9	3
Double Hamburger	320	15	6
CheeseBurger	270	12	5
Whopper Junior	300	16	4.5
TenderGrill Chicken Sandwich w/o Mayo	320	5	1
Chicken Nuggets, 4 pc *(BBQ, Teriyaki, & Jerk Sauces are low cal./fat)*	190	11	2
Big Fish Sandwich (without Tartar)	350	9	.5
Apples Slices	30	0	0
Fries, value menu	240	10	1.5
Onion Rings, value menu	150	8	1.5
Strawberry Sundae	190	4	2.5
Smoothie, Strawberry Banana, 12 oz.	190	5	0
Burger King NO!			
A1 Ultimate Bacon Cheeseburger	850	51	22
Double Whopper	900	56	19
BK Ultimate Breakfast Platter	1420	79	29
TenderCrisp Chicken Sandwich	640	36	6
Original Chicken Sandwich	640	36	6
Chick-fil-A YES!			
Chick-n-Minis, 3	280	10	3

cont'd next page

WELL, YES AND NO

RESTAURANT Chick-fil-A YES! (cont'd)	Total Calories	Total Fat (g)	Saturated Fat (g)
Multigrain Oatmeal w/fruit	140	3	0
Yogurt Parfait w/Granola	290	6	2
Grilled Chicken Sandwich	320	5	2
Chicken Sandwich	440	18	4
Grilled Chicken Cool Wrap	340	3	5
Chargrilled Chicken & Fruit Salad, no dressing	220	6	4
Chargrilled Chicken Garden Salad, no dressing	180	6	4
Southwest Chargrilled Chick. Salad, no dressing	240	9	4
Side Salad	80	5	3
Reduced Fat Berry Balsamic Vinaigrette, 1pkt	110	4	0
Hearty Breast of Chicken Soup, lrg	250	6	1
Icedream, cup	290	7	5
Icedream, cone	170	4	2
Chick-fil-A NO!			
Chick-n-Strips, 4 pc	470	24	4.5
Buttermilk Ranch or Caesar Dressing, 1pkt	280	30	5
Cole Slaw, sml	360	31	5
Cookies & Cream Milkshake, lrg	660	31	15
Dunkin Donuts YES!			
Onion Bagel	310	1	0

Bagels *between values listed*
    Blueberry, Cinnamon Raisin, Garlic,
    Plain, Sour Cream & Onion, Wheat
	320
	-350
		2.5
		-3.5
			2.5
			-3.5

Sesame Seed Bagel *(Poppy is 10cal. less)* *(If using cream cheese, go with reduced fat only.)*	350	4.5	1

WELL, YES AND NO

RESTAURANT Dunkin Donuts YES! (cont'd)	Total Calories	Total Fat (g)	Saturated Fat (g)
Egg & Cheese Wake-Up Wrap	150	8	3.5
Egg White Turkey Sausage Wake-Up Wrap	150	6	2.5
Egg White Veggie Wake-Up Wrap *(egg white flatbread sandwiches are good too)*	150	7	3
Egg & Cheese on English Muffin	240	7	3.5
Original Oatmeal w/dried fruit	270	4	1
Hash Browns, DD Smarts	130	7	1
Tuna Salad Sandwich on English Muffin	400	24	3.5
Turkey & Cheese Sandwich	460	14	6
Grilled Chicken Flatbread Sandwich	360	12	3.5
Blueberry Coffee, small, plain	15	0	0
Sugar Raised Donut *(better than glazed)* *most donuts average 300 cal. and 18 g. fat*	230	14	6
Glazed Munchkin, 1 *(others are similar)* *Remember though, that's for just one!*	70	4	2
Oatmeal Raisin Cookie	160	5	2.5
Dunkin Donuts NO!			
Salt Bagel, cal/fat are ok, BUT it has 3380mg. sodium!!!			
Chocolate Coconut Cake Donut	550	39	25
Coffee Cake Muffin	590	24	8
Tuna Melt on croissant	680	47	15
Chicken Salad on a Croissant	580	38	11
Einstein Bros. Bagels YES!			
"The Lighter Side" under 400 cal. breakfast & lunch menu			
Everything Thin Bagel *(Plain or Wheat are less)*	180	2	0

cont'd next page

WELL, YES AND NO

RESTAURANT Einstein Bros. Bagels YES! (cont'd)	Total Calories	Total Fat (g)	Saturated Fat (g)
Asiago Cheese Classic Bagel	290	4	2
All other Classic & Signature Flavor Bagels (between these values)	240 -300	1 -6	0 -2
Power Protein Bagel	290	5	.5
Nova Lox & Bagel	460	21	10
Light Plain Cream Cheese (better than reduced fat)	130	11	7
Veg Out Sandwich on Sesame Bagel	430	14	8
SW Turkey Sausage Sandwich, Eggwhite	390	13	6
Turkey and Cheddar Deli Sandwich	480	13	4
Albacore Tuna Salad Deli Sandwich	480	20	3
Chicken Salad Deli Sandwich	540	21	3
Open Face Turkey & Cheddar Deli Melt	500	15	8
Cheese Only Pizza Bagel	430	14	8
Chipotle Chicken Chopped Salad, Full	200	8	1
Chicken Noodle Soup, Bowl	180	5	.5
Einstein Bros. Bagels NO!			
Chipotle Turkey Wrap	640	29	12
Italian Chicken Panini	760	31	8
Chocolate Chip Coffee Cake	800	36	14
KFC YES!			
Orig. Recipe Chicken, Whole Wing	140	8	1.5
Orig. Recipe Chick. Breast, no skin/breading	130	2	.5
Orig. Recipe Chicken Drumstick	120	7	1.5
Orig. Recipe Chicken Thigh	290	21	5

WELL, YES AND NO

RESTAURANT KFC YES! (cont'd)	Total Calories	Total Fat (g)	Saturated Fat (g)
Grilled Chicken Breast	220	7	2
Grilled Chicken Drumstick	90	4	1
Grilled Chicken Thigh	170	10	3
Grilled Chicken Wing	80	4.5	1.5
Original Recipe Bites, 4 pc	130	6	1
Whole Kernel Corn, side	100	.5	0
Crispy Tenders, 2	250	13	1.5
Hot/Fiery Buffalo Hot Wings, 1	70	4	1
Honey BBQ Hot Wings, 1	80	4	1
Sweet & Sour Dipping Sauce	45	0	0
Honey BBQ Dipping Sauce	40	0	0
KFC Famous Bowl, snack-size	280	13	3.5
Crispy Chicken Caesar Salad, no dressing	330	18	4
Marzetti Light Italian Dressing	15	.5	0
Parmesan Garlic Croutons, 1 pouch	70	3	0
Green Beans, side	25	0	0
Mashed Potatoes with Gravy, side	120	4	1
Macaroni and Cheese, side	170	6	1.5
BBQ Baked Beans, side	210	1.5	0
Cole Slaw, side	170	10	1.5
Corn on the Cob, 3", side	70	.5	0
Lil' Bucket Strawberry Shortcake Parfait	200	7	3.5
Choc. Chip Cookie, 1 *(Oatmeal Raisin even better)*	160	8	3.5

cont'd next page

WELL, YES AND NO

RESTAURANT	Total Calories	Total Fat (g)	Saturated Fat (g)
KFC NO!			
Extra Crispy Chicken Breast	490	29	4.5
(Extra/Spicy Crispy items all high in cal./fat)			
Doublicious Sandwich, cheese & sauce	490	24	6
Crispy Twister, w/sauce	610	32	6
Chicken Pot Pie	790	45	38.5
KFC Famous Bowls, Mashed Potato w/Gravy	650	26	6
KFC Creamy Parmesan Caesar Dressing	260	26	5
Potato Wedges, side	290	15	2.5
Country Fried Steak w/Peppered White Gravy	390	26	7
Long John Silver's YES!			
"Freshside Grille" Entrees, as served			
Battered Alaskan Pollock, 1 pc *only*	230	14	5
Cranberry Walnut Chicken Salad, 1 salad	160	18	6
Baked Cod	160	1	0
Cocktail Sauce, 1oz.	25	0	0
Tartar Sauce, 1 packet	40	4	1
Hushpuppy, 2 pups	160	13	5
Corn Cobbette w/Butter Oil	150	10	2
Seasoned Green Beans	29	0	0
Rice, side	180	1	.5
Long John Silver's NO!			
Ciabatta Jack Chicken Sandwich	660	33	10
Battered Onion Rings, 5 pieces	350	26	10
Baja Fish Taco, 1	580	39	10

WELL, YES AND NO

RESTAURANT Long John Silver's NO! (cont'd)	Total Calories	Total Fat (g)	Saturated Fat (g)
Broccoli Cheese Soup, bowl	220	18	8
McDonald's YES!			
Egg White Delight McMuffin	250	8	3
Egg McMuffin	300	13	5
Hotcakes (using syrup *adds* 180cal./0fat)	350	9	2
Hash Brown	150	9	1.5
Southern Style Chicken Biscuit, lrg	470	24	9
Fruit & Maple Oatmeal, w/Brown Sugar	290	4.5	1.5
Hamburger	240	8	3
Cheeseburger	290	11	5
McDouble	380	17	8
Filet-O-Fish	390	19	4
Southern Style Crispy Chicken Sandwich	430	19	3
Premium Grilled Chicken Classic Sandwich	350	9	2
McChicken	360	16	3
Honey Mustard Snack Wrap, Crispy	340	16	4.5
Honey Mustard Snack Wrap, Grilled	260	9	3.5
Ranch Snack Wrap, Grilled	280	13	4.5
Chicken McNuggets, 6 (*use Hot Mustard, Sweet & Sour, or Buffalo sauce*)	280	18	3
Southwest Salad w/Grilled Chick., no dressing	290	8	2.5
Creamy S.West Dressing, 1.5oz *(Newman's)*	100	6	1
LowFat Balsamic Vinaigrette 1.5oz *(Newman's)*	35	2.5	0
LowFat Family Recipe Italian 1.5oz *(Newman's)*	50	2.5	.5

cont'd next page

WELL, YES AND NO

RESTAURANT McDonald's YES! (cont'd)	Total Calories	Total Fat (g)	Saturated Fat (g)
Apple Slices	15	0	0
Fruit 'n Yogurt Parfait (Caramel Apple is similar)	150	2	1
Strawberry Sundae	280	6	4
Hot Caramel Sundae (Hot Fudge is similar)	340	8	5
Choc. Chip Cookie, 1 (Oat. Raisin even better)	160	8	3.5
Baked Hot Apple Pie	250	13	7
McDonald's NO!			
Steak, Egg & Cheese Bagel	670	35	13
Double Quarter Pounder with Cheese	740	42	19
Premium McWrap SW Chicken, Crispy	670	32	8
Newman's Own Ranch Dressing, 1.5oz.	170	15	2.5
Chocolate McCafe Shake, 16oz.	700	20	12
McFlurry w/M&M'S Candies, 16oz.	930	33	20
Panera Bread YES!			
Asiago Cheese Bagel (Everything Bagel is less)	330	6	4
Chocolate Chip Bagel (Cinnamon Swirl & French Toast flavors are similar in cal./fat)	380	6	3
Whole Grain Bagel (Blueberry is slightly less)	340	3	0
Egg & Cheese on Ciabatta	390	15	7
Power Chicken Hummus Bowl, 1	270	10	1
"You Pick Two" small size soup options:			
Low Fat Natural Chicken & Noodle Soup*	80	1	0
Low Fat Garden Vegetable Soup w/Pesto*	90	4	0
Low Fat Vegetarian Black Bean Soup*	150	2	0
French Onion Soup w/croutons*	200	9	5

WELL, YES AND NO

RESTAURANT Panera Bread YES! (cont'd)	Total Calories	Total Fat (g)	Saturated Fat (g)
"You Pick Two" half sandwich options:			
Smokehouse Turkey Hot Panini	360	13	6
Smoked Turkey on Country Miche*	220	2	0
Chicken Salad on Sesame Semolina	340	12	1
Mediterranean Veggie on Tom. Basil*	280	6	2
Asiago Roast Beef on Asiago Cheese	390	17	8
"You Pick Two" half size salad options:			
Asian Sesame Chicken Salad, w/dressing*	210	11	2
BBQ Chopped Chicken Salad, w/dressing*	230	10	2
Thai Chopped Chicken Salad, w/dressing*	240	10	2
Classic Cafe Salad, w/dressing*	80	5	1
Greek Salad, no dressing*	80	16	4
*also good as full size, stand alone options			
Asian Sesame Vinaigrette, 3T	110	9	2
Low Fat Thai Chili Vinaigrette, 3T	50	2	0
Reduced Fat Balsamic Vinaigrette, 3T	130	11	2
Petite Cookies, 1, all have approximately	100	5	3
Panera Bread NO!			
Carrot Cake with Walnuts	650	26	9
Bear Claw	550	28	13
Frontega Chicken Panini	780	30	8
Steak & Blue Cheese Chop. Salad w/dressing	680	48	14
Signature Mac & Cheese, 16oz.	980	61	26
Quiznos YES!			
"Under 500 Calories" items, as served (*Roadhouse Steak/Cantina Chicken Sammies are under 300!*)			

cont'd next page

WELL, YES AND NO

RESTAURANT Quiznos YES! (cont'd)	Total Calories	Total Fat (g)	Saturated Fat (g)
Chili, bowl *(Chick. Noodle Soup is about half)*	280	6	1.5
Harvest Chicken Salad, no dressing, small	190	8	4
Veggie Sub, no cheese, no vinaigrette	460	16	3.5
Balsamic Vinaigrette, lrg	80	0	0
Oatmeal Raisin Cookie	360	12	7
Quiznos NO!			
Broccoli Cheese Bread Bowl, lrg	1030	41	15
Most Large subs are *MORE than*	1000	50	20
Schlotzsky's YES!			
Smoked Turkey Breast Sandwich, med	500	6	1
Chicken Breast Sandwich, med	490	3	0
Fresh Veggie Sandwich, med	500	14	7
Turkey & Guacamole Sandwich, med	520	11	3
Chicken & Pesto Sandwich, med	560	11	2
Dijon Chicken Sandwich, med	520	7	1
Angus Corned Beef Sandwich, med	510	9	2.5
Homestyle Tuna Sandwich, sml	390	11	2
Chipotle Chicken Sandwich	530	9	1
Smoked Turkey Breast Wrap, med	450	14	3
Chipotle Chicken Wrap	480	16	3
Chicken Breast Wrap, med	440	10	3
Fresh Veggie Wrap, med	460	20	8
Fresh Veggie Gourmet Pizza 14", 2 slices	440	18	6
Chicken Tortilla Soup, bowl	300	15	7

WELL, YES AND NO

RESTAURANT	Total Calories	Total Fat (g)	Saturated Fat (g)
Schlotzsky's YES! (cont'd)			
Veggie Vegetable Soup, bowl	130	0	0
Timberline Chili, bowl	450	22	9
Garden Salad, no dressing	40	2	0
Fat Free Raspberry Vinaigrette, 3oz.	99	0	0
Schlotzsky's Balsamic Vinegar Dressing, 3T	15	0	0
Pasta Salad	68	3	0
Fudge, or Reg., Chocolate Chip Cookie, 1 (*Oatmeal/Sugar/Macadamia are similar*)	160	7	4
Schlotzsky's NO!			
Try not to eat the bag of chips, they add about	230	15	2
Albuquerque Turkey Sandwich, med	860	37	15
Deluxe Original-Style Sandwich, med	980	46	18
Chicken Chipotle Pesto Flatbread	790	49	12
Cheesy Bacon Soup, bowl	510	41	20
Carrot Cake, 1 pc	717	42	6
Starbucks YES!			
Be sure to use skim milk, a sugar substitute, and no whipped cream in beverages.			
Greek Yogurt Honey Parfait	260	4.5	1
Fruit (various) Yogurt Parfait are *approx.*	310	4	.5
Blueberry Yogurt Muffin	320	13	3
Reduced Fat Very Berry Coffee Cake, 1 pc	320	11	3.5
Michigan Cherry Oat Bar	240	8	5
Starbucks Perfect Oatmeal	160	2.5	.5
Spinach, Feta, Egg White Breakfast Wrap	290	10	3.5

cont'd next page

WELL, YES AND NO

RESTAURANT Starbucks YES! (cont'd)	Total Calories	Total Fat (g)	Saturated Fat (g)
Turkey Bacon/White Cheddar Breakfast Sand.	230	6	2.5
Vegetable & Fontiago Breakfast Sand.	470	17	7
Spinach & Feta Breakfast Wrap	290	10	3.5
Chicken & Hummus Bistro Box	270	7	0
Chicken Santa Fe Panini	410	12	6
Protein Bistro Box	380	19	6
Hearty Veggie & Brown Rice Salad Bowl	430	22	3
Holiday Turkey & Stuffing Panini	440	10	4
Roasted Tomato & Mozzarella Panini	390	18	6
Zesty Chicken & Black Bean Salad Bowl	360	15	2.5
Flourless Cherry Chocolate Cookie	170	4.5	2.5
Pumpkin Bread, 1 pc	410	15	3
Petite Vanilla Bean Scone most other "Petite" items are *around*	120 180	4.5 9	2 5
Starbucks NO!			
Cheese Danish	320	16	9
Mallorca Sweet Bread, 1	460	27	13
Raspberry Scone	420	17	10
Iced Lemon Pound Cake	470	20	9
Egg Salad Sandwich	500	28	5

Peppermint White Choc. Mocha Espresso,
    20oz. w/whole milk & whipped cream
    (it also has 24 teaspoons of sugar!)
	680	26	17

Subway YES!			
Subway's "6 grams of fat or less" are good choices			

WELL, YES AND NO

RESTAURANT Subway YES! (cont'd)	Total Calories	Total Fat (g)	Saturated Fat (g)
Egg White & Cheese Flatbread, 3"	170	5	1.5
Steak, Egg White & Cheese, 3"	190	6	2
Egg & Cheese Omelet Sandwich, 6"	360	12	4.5
Steak, Egg & Cheese Omelet Sandwich, 6"	430	15	5
Reg. Egg & Cheese Flatbread, 3"	190	7	2.5
Steak, Reg. Egg and Cheese Flatbread, 3"	210	8	3
Chicken Noodle Soup 8oz. bowl *(Tomato Garden, Minestrone & Veg. Beef are similar)*	110	3	.5
Black Bean Soup, 1 bowl	210	0	0
Creamy Chick. & Dumplings Soup, 8oz. bowl	150	4.5	2
Minestrone Soup, 8oz. bowl	90	1	0
Thai Coconut Soup, 1 bowl	210	3	0
6" Sandwiches, 9-grain, no mayo/dressing: *(Flatbread versions are similar in cal./fat.)*			
Oven Roasted Chicken or Roast Beef	320	5	1.5
Sweet Onion Chicken Teriyaki	370	4.5	1
Turkey Breast	280	3.5	1
Veggie Delite	230	2.5	.5
Big Philly Cheesesteak	500	17	9
Meatball Marinara	480	18	7
Steak & Cheese	380	10	4.5
6" Buffalo Chicken, 9-grain w/Ranch dressing	420	16	3
Footlong Veggie Delite	460	5	1
Roast Beef Salad, no dressing	140	3.5	1

cont'd next page

WELL, YES AND NO

RESTAURANT Subway YES! (cont'd)	Total Calories	Total Fat (g)	Saturated Fat (g)
Oven Roasted Chick. Breast Salad, no dressing	130	2.5	.5
Sweet Onion Chick. Teriyaki Salad, w/dressing	200	3	1
Turkey Breast Salad, no dressing	110	2	.5
Veggie Delite Salad, no dressing	110	1	0
Apple Slices-1 package	35	0	0
Choc. Chip Cookie, 1 *(Oat. Raisin even better)*	220	10	5
Subway NO!			
6" Big Hot Pastrami Sandwich	580	31	11
6" Tuna on 9-Grain Wheat Bread	480	25	5
Footlong Sweet Onion Chicken Teriyaki	740	9	2
Big Hot Pastrami Melt Salad	400	29	11
Ranch Dressing, 2 oz	320	35	6
Taco Bell YES!			
Fresco Crunchy Taco (beef)	150	8	2.5
Crunchy Taco (beef)	170	10	3.5
Soft Taco (beef)	190	9	4
Soft Taco Supreme (beef)	220	11	5
Double Decker Taco (beef)	320	14	5
Fresco Chicken Soft Taco	140	3.5	1
Chicken Soft Taco	160	5	2.5
Grilled Steak Soft Taco	200	10	3.5
Crispy Potato Soft Taco	250	13	3
Gordita Supreme-Chicken	270	9	3.5
Black Beans & Rice	180	4	0

WELL, YES AND NO

RESTAURANT Taco Bell YES! (cont'd)	Total Calories	Total Fat (g)	Saturated Fat (g)
Bean Burrito	370	10	4
Beef Burrito Supreme	410	16	7
Chicken Burrito Supreme	390	12	5
Steak Burrito Supreme	400	13	5
Grilled Chicken Burrito	400	18	4.5
Chicken Chalupa Supreme	350	18	4
Steak Chalupa Supreme	350	19	4.5
Mexican Rice, side	100	2.5	0
Pintos 'n Cheese, side	190	7	3
Reduced Fat Sour Cream	60	3.5	2.5
Guacamole	70	6	1
Jalapeno *or* Pepper Jack Sauce (*Border Sauce or Salsa saves about 50cal./7g. fat*)	70	7	1
Cinnamon Twists, side	170	7	0
Taco Bell NO!			
1/2 lb. Cheesy Potato Burrito	510	24	7
XXL Grilled Stuft Burrito (beef)	870	41	14
XXL Steak Nacho	1190	60	11
Fiesta Taco Salad-Steak	750	37	8
Chicken Fiesta Taco Salad	740	35	7
Wendy's YES!			
Jr. Hamburger	240	9	3.5
Jr. Cheeseburger	280	12	6
Garden Side Salad, no dressing	110	3	.5

cont'd next page

WELL, YES AND NO

RESTAURANT Wendy's YES! (cont'd)	Total Calories	Total Fat (g)	Saturated Fat (g)
Ultimate Chicken Grill Sandwich	370	7	1.5
Crispy Chicken Sandwich	350	19	3.5
Grilled Chicken Go Wrap	270	10	3.5
Spicy Chicken Wrap	340	16	5
Chicken Nuggets, 6 (BBQ or Sweet & Sour Sauce adds about 50cal.)	270	18	4
Apple Pecan Chicken Salad, half size, w/roasted pecans	280	15	5
Spicy Chicken Caesar Salad, half size, no dressing	330	16	6
Pomegranate Vinaigrette, 1 pkt	70	3	0
Light Asian Vinaigrette, 1 pkt	45	1.5	0
Plain Baked Potato, average 10oz.	270	0	0
Sour Cream & Chives Baked Potato	320	3.5	2
Chili, lrg	250	7	3
Apple Slices	40	0	0
Chocolate Frosty, sml	340	9	6
Vanilla Frosty, sml	330	8	5
Wendy's NO!			
1/2 lb. Double	820	47	20
Spicy Chicken Caesar Salad, w/dressing	780	51	16
Asiago Ranch Chicken Club	670	32	9
Thousand Island Dressing, 1 pkt	130	12	1.5

ALL AMERICAN

You say you don't do fast foods? Many believe that the more traditional sit-down restaurants are a healthier choice. They certainly have that reputation, especially compared to food that comes in a bag. While places like Applebee's, Denny's, and Chili's often don't do much better nutritionally than most drive-thru's, they can provide you with a greater choice of healthier alternatives.

COMFORT FOOD?	Total Calories	Total Fat (g)	Sat. Fat (g)
Denny's Brooklyn Spag. & Meatballs	1220	61	21
Johnny Rocket's Grilled Cheese	520	31	16
Denny's Country Fried Steak w/gravy	760	47	15
Bob Evan's Meat Loaf, 7.5oz.	345	23	9
Denny's Apple Pie, 7oz.	480	22	9

Many choices at sit-down restaurants remind us of the food we grew up on. However, those "comfortable" foods may not be that good for you.

ALL YOU CAN EAT?

SURPRISE! *Buffets like Golden Corral and Old Country/Hometown Buffet can be a good choice. You'd think they'd be a nutritionist's nightmare,*  *but they also offer an abundance of fresh fruits and vegetables, salads, and seafood. Yes, you can overindulge on the dessert bar and research shows that for many people the more food that's offered, the more they consume. If you know you can't handle the abundant offerings, then a more traditional order-from-the-menu place with controlled portions is the way to go.*

MAKING GOOD CHOICES	Total Calories	Total Fat (g)	Saturated Fat (g)
AT GOLDEN CORRAL TRY:			
Salmon, Whole Carved, 3oz.	120	6	1.5
INSTEAD OF:			
Smothered Chopped Steak, 1	320	20	8
OR Awesome, Pot Roast, 3oz.	100	7	3
INSTEAD OF:			
Lasagna, 1 piece	430	26	13
AT OLD COUNTRY BUFFET TRY:			
Chicken & Dumplings, 1 spoon	160	5	1
INSTEAD OF:			
BBQ Beef Ribs, 1 serving	300	23	9
OR Waldorf Salad, 1 spoon	110	7	1
INSTEAD OF:			
Macaroni Vegetable Salad, 1 spoon	240	16	3

WELL, YES AND NO

RESTAURANT Applebee's YES!	Total Calories	Total Fat (g)	Saturated Fat (g)
"Under 600" items (see cal./fat on menu)			
Lunch Combo items: French Onion Soup	370	23	14
Tomato Basil Soup	240	15	7
Chicken Tortilla Soup	220	9	2.5
Caesar Salad w/dressing	210	18	4
Oriental Chicken Salad w/dressing	440	29	4.5
Chicken Wonton Tacos	480	14	3
Classic Turkey Breast Sandwich	280	14	2
House Sirloin, 7oz, no sides	280	15	6
Baked Potato, plain	278	0	0
Seasonal Vegetables	60	0	0
Sweet Potato Fries	340	12	2
Grilled Chicken Caesar Salad w/dressing, 1/2	400	28	6
Grilled Chicken Wonton Tacos	360	11	2
Steak & Honey BBQ Chicken Combo, no sides	620	18	7
Veggie Burger, no sides	550	24	4.5
Blackened Tilapia	450	17	5
Pepper-Crusted Sirloin & Whole Grains	350	9	2.5
Savory Cedar Salmon	520	28	8
Dijon Honey Mustard Dressing	210	18	2.5
Brownie Bite	380	18	9
Hot Fudge Sundae Shooter	460	22	15
Strawberry Cheesecake Shooter	390	24	14

cont'd next page

WELL, YES AND NO

RESTAURANT *Applebee's NO!*	Total Calories	Total Fat (g)	Saturated Fat (g)
Cheeseburger Sliders, no fries	1690	103	32
Quesadilla Burger, no fries	1420	108	45
Chick. Tenders & Riblet Platter, Smoky Chip.	1820	108	27
Pecan-Crusted Chick. Salad w/dress, reg.	1340	80	16
Sizzling Skillet Fajitas-Steak	1360	52	24
New England Fish & Chips	1970	136	24
Blue Ribbon Brownie	1670	78	40
Chili's YES!			
Southwest Chicken Soup, bowl	230	10	2
Terlingua Chili w/Toppings, cup	200	14	4
Lighter Choice Classic Sirloin, w/sides	240	7	3
Lighter Choice Salmon, w/sides	540	24	4
Grilled Salmon w/Garlic & Herbs	400	26	6
Lighter Choice Margarita Grilled Chick., w/sides	610	16	3
Caribbean Salad w/grilled Chicken, w/dress	680	27	4.5
Mango-Chile Tilapia	520	17	3.5
Chicken Fajitas, no tortillas or condiments	410	25	6
w/tortillas, 3, *add*	260	9	4
House Salad, no dressing	70	3	1.5
Black Beans, side	110	.5	0
Cinnamon Apples, side *(eat them for dessert!)*	270	11	3.5
Chili's NO!			
Classic Beef Nachos, lrg appetizer	1590	103	51
Hot Spinach & Artichoke Dip w/chips	1440	91	35

WELL, YES AND NO

RESTAURANT Chili's NO! (cont'd)	Total Calories	Total Fat (g)	Saturated Fat (g)
Quesadilla Explosion Salad, w/dressing	1430	95	28
Smokehouse Burger	1550	89	29
Skillet Toffee Fudge Brownie	1240	62	34
Denny's YES!			
"Fit Fare" items (see cal./fat on menu)			
Turkey Bacon Strips, 4	100	7	2
Egg Whites, 2	50	0	0
English Muffin, no margarine	140	1	0
Grits w/margarine, 12oz.	220	3	1
Oatmeal w/Milk & Brown Sugar	240	5	1.5
Low Fat Yogurt, 6oz.	160	1.5	1
Hearty Wheat Pancakes, 2 w/Maple-Flavored syrup (3 tbsp) add	310 100	1.5 0	0 0
Harvest Oatmeal Breakfast	530	11	5
Chicken Avocado Sandwich w/veggies	490	11	4
Cranberry Apple Chicken Salad, w/balsamic vinaigrette, no bread	450	14	3
Vegetable Beef Soup, bowl	168	4	1
Chicken Noodle Soup, bowl	140	4	2
Mashed Potatoes, 4oz. side (broccoli, corn, spinach, fruit, etc. are good, too)	100	3	2
Whole Grain Rice	227	4	0
Denny's NO!			
The Grand Slamwich w/hash browns	1340	89	28

cont'd next page

WELL, YES AND NO

RESTAURANT **Denny's NO!** (cont'd)	Total Calories	Total Fat (g)	Saturated Fat (g)
Santa Fe Skillet	710	52	15
Meat Lover's Omelette w/Hash Browns	1020	73	23
Loaded Baked Potato Soup, 12 oz.	420	32	16
Bourbon Bacon Burger w/fries	1540	86	27
Golden Corral YES!			
French Toast, plain, 1 slice *Save cal., use fruit topping/yogurt not syrup.*	200	6	1.5
Peach Fruit Topping, 2 Tbsp *(other fruit toppings are similar)*	35	0	0
Pancakes, plain, 2 *(Blueberry 10cal. more)*	160	8	2
Crepes, Strawberry, 1 *(Cherry 10cal. more)*	120	4	1
Waffle, 1	70	0	0
Grits, 1/2 cup	110	2.5	.5
Salad Bar, *go mostly veggies and fruit*			
Broccoli Salad, 1/2 cup	110	8	1.5
Carrot Raisin Salad, 1/2 cup	110	7	1
Marinated Vegetable Salad, 1/2 cup	35	2	0
Cottage Cheese, 1/2 cup	90	2.5	1.5
Garbanzo Beans, 1/4 cup	60	1	0
Lite Olive Oil Vinaigrette, 2 Tbsp.	70	6	1
Fat Free Ranch, 2 Tbsp. *(other Fat Free dressings are similar cal.)*	35	0	0
Chicken & Pasta Soup, 1 cup	90	4	1
Vegetable Beef Soup, 1 cup	80	1	0
Spring Roll, 1	60	3.5	.5

WELL, YES AND NO

RESTAURANT Golden Corral YES! (cont'd)	Total Calories	Total Fat (g)	Saturated Fat (g)
Awesome Pot Roast, 3oz.	160	7	3
Beef Tips, marinated, 3oz.	140	5	1.5
Sirloin Steak, 3 oz.	150	6	3
Rotisserie Chicken, breast & wing, w/skin	310	15	4.5
Turkey Breast w/Wing, 3oz.	70	3	1
Chicken Breast, 1 piece	100	2.5	0
Chicken & Pastry Noodles, 1/2 cup	100	5	1.5
Salmon, whole carved, 3oz.	120	6	1.5
Jalapeno Glazed Tilapia, 1	170	8	1.5
Roast Beef, 3oz.	110	3	1
Salisbury Steak, 1 each	130	4.5	1.5
Macaroni & Cheese, 1/2 cup	190	9	3.5
Rice Pilaf, 1/2 cup	150	5	1
Red Bliss Potatoes, 1/2 cup	80	2	0
Mashed Potatoes, 1/2 cup	160	8	1.5
2oz. poultry or brown gravy *adds about*	25	.5	0
Southern Style Northern/Pinto Beans, 1/2 cup	170	4	1.5
Green Bean Casserole, 1/2 cup	80	4.5	1
Corn, cut kernel, 1/2 cup	100	2	0
Steamed Broccoli, Cauliflower, Green Beans 1/2 cup, all *around or under*	35	0	0
Apple Cobbler, 1 pc *(other fruits are similar)*	150	5	2
Apple Pie, 1 slice *(cherry is similar)*	330	13	5
Note: Sugar Free Desserts are usually better than "No Sugar Added"			

cont'd next page

WELL, YES AND NO

RESTAURANT Golden Corral YES! (cont'd)	Total Calories	Total Fat (g)	Saturated Fat (g)
Blueberry Pie, No Sugar Added, 1 slice	280	8	3
Bread Pudding, 1/2 cup	270	13	7
Brownie, 1	140	6	1.5
Chocolate Covered Banana w/Peanuts, 1	160	9	5
Chocolate Chip Cookie, 1	60	3	1
Orange Sherbet, 1/2 cup	110	1	.5
Soft Serve, Choc., 1/2 cup (vanilla–add 20cal.)	90	2	1.5
Lemon Bars, 1 pc	150	4	1.5
Strawberry Shortcake, 1 pc	120	4.5	1.5
Golden Corral NO!			
Blueberry Muffin, 1	450	28	6
Chicken Salad, 1/2 cup	240	20	3
Macaroni Salad, 1/2 cup	280	22	3
Smothered Chopped Steak, 1	320	20	8
Patty Melt, 1 piece	380	22	8
BBQ Chicken Leg Quarter, 1	490	22	9
Lasagna, 1 pc	430	26	13
Homemade Italian Meatballs, 2	140	16	5
Stuffed Pepper, 1	170	19	6
Spinach, creamed, 1/2 cup	230	18	4
Peach Pie, No Sugar Added, 1 slice	330	21	9
Carrot Cake, 1 slice	290	15	4.5
Chocolate Chess Pie, 1 slice	380	19	7
Peanut Butter Mini Cream Tart, 1	340	21	6

WELL, YES AND NO

RESTAURANT IHOP YES!	Total Calories	Total Fat (g)	Saturated Fat (g)
"Simple & Fit" under 600 calories breakfast, lunch, & dinner menu items			
Ask for vanilla yogurt or applesauce as a pancake/waffle topping.			
Original Buttermilk Pancakes, 3	470	15	5
Blueberry Fruit Crepe	460	16	7
Double Blueberry Pancakes, 3, side	540	13	4.5
Original Buttermilk Pancakes, 3, side	470	15	5
Strawberry Banana Pancakes, 3, side	600	13	4.5
Belgian Waffle, plain	500	24	14
Create Your Own Omelette, egg substitute only	140	4	.5
w/American or Swiss Cheese, *add* (*not using Cheddar saves 80cal./7fat*)	160	13	8
w/Fresh Tomatoes, *add* (*spinach, peppers, etc. add very few calories*)	10	0	0
Turkey Bacon Strips, 4, add-on	150	11	3
Turkey Sausage Links, 4, add-on	180	10	2.5
Chicken Noodle Soup	170	6	2.5
Minestrone Soup	150	2.5	0
Turkey Sandwich, 1/2	290	18	4.5
Honey-Lime Chicken Salad	410	21	4
House Salad w/Reduced Fat Italian Dressing	40	1.5	0
Mixed Greens House Salad w/ French	110	1	
Seasonal Fresh Fruit	6	0	0
Vanilla Ice Cream, 1 scoop (*Chocolate and Strawberry are similar*)	90	5	3.5

cont'd next page

WELL, YES AND NO

RESTAURANT IHOP NO!	Total Calories	Total Fat (g)	Saturated Fat (g)
Cinnamon Swirl French Toast Combo	1220	70	19
Pick-A-Pancake Combo, Harvest Grain 'N Nut	1070	75	21
Chicken Clubhouse Super Stacker	1150	76	25
Country Omelette	1180	88	31
Chicken Fajita Omelette	1050	74	26
Turkey Berry Melt	1200	68	34
Bacon & White Cheddar Melt, Full Sand.	1610	113	48
Side Caesar Salad w/dressing	380	33	7
LongHorn Steakhouse YES!			
Longhorn Salmon, 7oz. lunch size*	300	16	3
French Onion Soup, cup	215	14	6
Mixed Greens Salad, side, no dressing	100	4.5	1.5
Light Ranch Dressing, 1.5oz.	60	5	1

Grilled Chicken & Strawberry Salad,
    w/Vinaigrette, whole
    OR, w/regular dressing, half
	530
	280
		19
		11
			7
			2.5

Spinach Fetta Chicken	220	6	2
Balsamic-Raspberry Seared Chicken	450	20	7
Renegade Top Sirloin, 8oz. dinner size*	390	16	6
Longhorn Salmon, 10oz. dinner size*	430	23	4
Sweet Potato, no butter, side w/cinnamon sugar, add	240 30	1 0	0 0
Fresh Vegetables, side (asparagus is similar)	90	4	1
Seasoned Rice Pilaf, side	300	7	3

*No sides included.

WELL, YES AND NO

RESTAURANT LongHorn Steakhouse NO!	Total Calories	Total Fat (g)	Saturated Fat (g)
Parmesan Crusted Chicken, dinner size*	910	55	20
Longhorn Porterhouse, dinner size*	1130	69	29
Chop Steak, dinner size*	660	45	15
Chocolate Stampede, 1/2 (!)	1215	65	37
Caramel Apple Goldrush	1640	71	25
Old Country Buffet YES! (Note: 1 spoon is not a "heaping" spoon)			
Cinnamon Bread, 1 slice	160	2.5	.5
Cinnamon Roll, 1	140	5	1
Buttermilk Pancake, 1	110	2	.5
Waffle, 1	120	6	3
Poached Egg, 1	70	5	1.5
Scrambled Eggs, 1 spoon	120	10	2.5
Oatmeal, 4oz. (grits have same cal./0fat)	60	1.5	0
Potatoes O'Brien, 1 spoon	150	6	1
Fresh Fruit, all types, 1 spoon	25-60	0	0
Dinner Roll, 1 white (Cornbread is 10cal. more)	130	5	1
Chicken Noodle/Rice Soup, 1 (4oz.) ladle (French Onion/Veg. Beef are even less cal.)	80	2	.5
Chili Bean Soup, 1 (4oz.) ladle	80	3.5	1.5
Bruschetta Tomato Salad, 1 spoon	70	5	1
California Coleslaw, 1 spoon	100	0	0
Potato Salad, 1 spoon, all types, *approx.*	120	7	1
Three Bean Salad, 1 spoon	90	4.5	.5

cont'd next page

WELL, YES AND NO

RESTAURANT Old Country Buffet YES! (cont'd)	Total Calories	Total Fat (g)	Saturated Fat (g)
Waldorf Salad, 1 spoon	110	7	1
Make salads with mostly fresh veggies and Fat Free, Low or Reduced Fat Dressings			
Marinated Vegetables, 1 spoon	50	3.5	.5
Mashed Potatoes, 1 spoon	70	.5	0
Green Bean Casserole, 1 spoon	100	7	2.5
Candied Yams, 1 spoon	140	1.5	0
1 spoon of most other vegetables are *under* (BUT *most veg. casseroles are much more*)	100	5	2
Bread Dressing, 1 spoon	150	6	1
Cajun Rice, 1 spoon *(Veg. Rice Pilaf even less)*	90	2	0
Macaroni & Cheese, 1 spoon	110	2.5	1
Spaghetti & Meatballs, 1 spoon	140	5	2
Cheese Pizza, 1 slice	150	4	2
Chicken & Dumplings, 1 spoon	160	5	1
Chicken Zucchini Stir Fry, 1 spoon	100	3.5	1
Beef & Broccoli Stir-Fry 1 spoon	110	5	1.5
Roasted Jerk Chicken Breast, 1	320	18	5
Roasted Jerk Chicken Drumstick, 1	100	7	2
Roasted Jerk Chicken Thigh, 1	180	11	3
Traditional Baked & Rotisserie Style Chicken are similar to above. Save cal./fat by removing skin.			
Sizzling BBQ Brisket, 3oz.	170	6	2
Salisbury Steak, 1 pc	150	9	3.5
Carved Salmon Filet, 3oz.	190	11	2

WELL, YES AND NO

RESTAURANT Old Country Buffet YES! (cont'd)	Total Calories	Total Fat (g)	Saturated Fat (g)
Baked Fish, 1 pc	90	4.5	1
Roasted Rotisserie Style Turkey, 3oz.	100	4	1
Taco Shell, 1	50	2.5	.5
Flour Tortilla, 1	120	3	.5
Taco Meat, 1 spoon, Chicken/Beef	70/50	3	1
Refried Beans, 1 spoon	80	2.5	1.5
Steak Fajita, 1 spoon (Chicken has 12g. fat!)	120	6	2
Apple Crisp, 1 spoon (Cherry is similar)	160	3	.5
Bread Pudding, 1 spoon	180	7	3
Peach Cobbler, 1 spoon	210	8	2
Apple Spice Cake, 1 pc (BlackForest Cake has 30 cal. less)	180	7	1
Fudge Brownie, 1	200	6	1.5
Lemon Meringue or Cream Pie, 1 slice	130	4.5	1.5
Vanilla Pudding, 1 spoon (Choc. is 1g. fat less)	130	5	1
Frozen Nonfat Yogurt, Orange Sherbet, 4oz.	90	0	0
Chocolate Chip Cookie, 1 (Snickerdoodle is less)	130	6	2
Old Country Buffet NO!			
Garlic cheese Biscuit, 1	230	15	4
Macaroni Vegetable Salad, 1 spoon	240	16	3
Seven Layer Salad, 1 spoon	190	17	4.5
BBQ Beef Ribs 1 serving	300	23	9
Enchilada, 1	250	18	9
Blue Cheese Dressing, 1oz.	150	16	3

cont'd next page

WELL, YES AND NO

RESTAURANT Old Country Buffet NO! (cont'd)	Total Calories	Total Fat (g)	Saturated Fat (g)
White Cupcake, Decorated	310	16	4
Pecan Pie, 1 slice	310	19	4
Sweet Potato Pie, 1 pc	280	18	4.5
Outback Steakhouse YES!			
"Under 600 Calories" items, as served			
Grilled Chicken on the Barbie, lunch	198	2	0
Grilled Salmon, no sides	390	25	4
Outback Special (steak), 6oz., no sides	254	13	5
Victoria Filet, 8oz., no sides	301	12	5
Steamed Broccoli, side *(Mixed Veggies, less fat)*	137	9	4
Fresh Steamed Green Beans, side *(Grilled Asparagus is similar in cal./fat)*	55	3	1
Seasoned Rice, side	260	0	0
Sweet Potato, plain, side	318	5	1
Baked Potato, plain, side	230	1	0
House Salad, side, no dressing w/Tangy Tomato Dressing, *add*	110 57	6 12	3 3
Carrot Cake, 1/2 pc	321	15	5
Classic Cheesecake, whole pc	321	15	5
Outback Steakhouse NO!			
Bloomin' Onion, 1/4 appetizer	487	40	12
Baked Potato Soup, cup	460	31	17
The Bloomin' Burger, no fries	1027	70	31
Ribeye, 14oz., no sides	762	49	21
No Rules Grilled Chicken Parmesan Pasta	1303	69	38

WELL, YES AND NO

RESTAURANT Outback Steakhouse NO! (cont'd)	Total Calories	Total Fat (g)	Saturated Fat (g)
Aussie Cobb w/Crispy Chicken, no dressing	850	52	24
Chocolate Thunder From Down Under, 1/2	787	54	28
Red Lobster YES!			
Bar Harbor Salad w/chicken	320	11	1.5
Baked Potato w/sour cream	225	2.5	1.5
Fresh Fish Grilled or Broiled, full dnr size no sides, *all types except Tilapia, Char, Salmon, and Trout which are more*	370 or less	4 or less	2 or less
Grilled Salmon, full dnr size, no sides	680	40	8
Grilled/Broiled Flounder, full dnr size, no sides *(Grouper is 20cal. more)*	340	8	0
Canadian Walleye, Blackened	220	4.5	.5
Grilled Sirloin, full dnr size, no sides	240	9	4
Wild Rice Pilaf, side	170	3	.5
Homestyle Mashed Potatoes, side	210	10	6
Asparagus, side	60	3.5	2.5
Fresh Broccoli, side	50	.5	0
Garden Salad, side, no dressing	70	1.5	0
Blueberry Balsamic Dressing	80	4	.5
Red Wine Balsamic Vinaigrette, 1.5oz.	80	5	0
Red Lobster NO!			
Cheddar Bay Biscuit, just 1	160	10	3
Battered Fried Walleye, full dnr size, no sides	1170	73	7
Hand-Tossed Caesar Dinner Salad	540	50	9
Chocolate Wave, 1	1490	81	25

cont'd next page

WELL, YES AND NO

RESTAURANT Ruby Tuesday YES!	Total Calories	Total Fat (g)	Saturated Fat (g)
CAUTION: Saturated fat is the most dangerous kind of fat. Ruby Tuesday has chosen not to publish this information.			
"Fit & Trim" items, as served, see cal./fat on menu and choose items *close to, or under* (Salad dressing cal./fat are not included in the nutritional values listed on their menu)	500	30	n/a
BBQ Chicken Flatbread, 1/2 appetizer	65	3	n/a
Chicken Tortilla Soup	166	7	n/a
Balsamic Vinaigrette Dressing	40	2	n/a
Lite Ranch Dressing	70	5	n/a
Petite Sirloin	284	19	n/a
Grilled Chicken, plain, no sides	190	5	n/a
Grilled Chicken Wrap, no sides	493	17	n/a
Herb-Crusted Tilapia, no sides	401	24	n/a
Chicken Bella, no sides	332	15	n/a
Hickory Bourbon Chicken, no sides	250	5	n/a
For Sides and Fit & Trim vegetable options, see menu or ask			
Rice Pilaf, side	160	3	n/a
White Chocolate Macadamia Nut Cookie, 1	200	12	n/a
Ruby Tuesday NO!			
Parmesan Chicken Pasta	1283	67	n/a
Spicy Jalapeno Pretzel Cheeseburger	1621	98	n/a
Chicken & Broccoli Pasta, no sides	1436	87	n/a
Ribs & Chicken Tenders	1295	60	n/a

WELL, YES AND NO

RESTAURANT	Total Calories	Total Fat (g)	Saturated Fat (g)
Ruby Tuesday NO! (cont'd)			
Loaded Baked Potato, side	561	35	n/a
Baked Mac 'n Cheese, side	465	28	n/a
New York Cheese Cake	758	60	n/a
Sizzler YES!			
Make salads with mostly fresh veggies and Fat Free, Low or Reduced Fat Dressings			
Ambrosia Salad, 4oz. spoon	123	4	4
Carrot Raisin Salad, 4oz. spoon	100	6	1
Creamy Cole Slaw, 2oz. tongful	34	2	0
Greek Salad, 4oz. spoon	50	4	1
Asian Chopped Salad, 4oz	30	2	0
Spinach Cranberry Salad, 4oz. spoon	45	3	0
Three Bean Salad, 1oz. spoon	25	1	0
Chicken Noodle or Tortilla Soup, 6oz. bowl	100	2-4	0
Minestrone Soup, 6oz. bowl *(Veg. is even less)*	68	1	0
Vegetable Steak Soup, 6oz. bowl	110	6	1
Hibachi Chicken, single	239	4	0
Lemon Herb Chicken, single	172	6	0
Italian Herb Chicken, 7oz.	292	16	7
Grilled Salmon w/Rice Pilaf	532	20	6
Classic Steak, 8oz.	393	21	8
Steak & Hibachi Chicken Combo	534	20	6
Steak & Lemon Herb Chicken Combo	491	24	8
Vegetable Medley, 5oz. side	80	4	2.5

cont'd next page

WELL, YES AND NO

RESTAURANT Sizzler YES! (cont'd)	Total Calories	Total Fat (g)	Saturated Fat (g)
Sautéed Spinach	105	7	1
Yeast Roll, 1	164	1	0
Rice Pilaf, 5oz. side	224	5	2
Mexican Rice, 3oz. spoon	116	2	0
Cilantro Lime Rice, 5oz.	116	0	0
Taco Meat, 1 *small* 1oz. spoon	61	3	1
Taco Shell, corn, 1	70	2	0
Nacho Cheese Sauce, 1oz. ladle	30	1	0
Banana Pudding, 4oz. spoon	224	9	7
Chocolate Mousse, 4oz. spoon	238	10	0
Hot Bread Pudding, 4oz. spoon	276	10	4
Chocolate/Vanilla Soft Serve, 1 serving	100	23	2.5
Pound Cake, 1 pc	161	6	3
Sizzler NO!			
Cheese Toast, 1 slice	237	19	9
Potato Salad, 4oz. spoon	325	27	5
Tuna Pasta Salad, 4oz. spoon	207	19	3
Mega Bacon Cheeseburger, ½ lb.	1008	61	27
Sizzler Burger, 1/2 lb.	760	40	15
Ribeye, 14oz.	1055	66	25
Loaded Baked Potato	454	22	11
UNO Chicago Grill YES!			
Walnut/Goat Cheese Salad w/dress, lunch size	230	17	5
Honey Citrus Salad w/dressing, lunch size	310	15	1.5

WELL, YES AND NO

RESTAURANT UNO Chicago Grill YES!	Total Calories	Total Fat (g)	Saturated Fat (g)
Power Salad w/dressing, reg size *(lunch size is about half the cal./fat)*	540	11	3.5
House Salad w/Grilled Chicken, no dressing	310	12	2.5
Garden Salad, no dressing, side	90	5	1
Fat Free Vinaigrette 2oz.	30	0	0
Low Fat Blueberry/Pomegr. Vinaigrette, 2oz.	120	6	1
"Small" Plate Items:			
Roasted Eggplant, Spinach & Feta Pasta	400	15	4.5
Mediterranean Farro Salad	270	18	6
Grilled Citrus Chicken Salad	570	26	4
Chicken Thumb Platter	480	17	3
Beef Barley Soup, 8oz. *(Veggie and Minestrone are similar cal./fat)*	140	2	.5
Cuban Black Bean & Lentil Soup, 8oz.	220	4.5	0
Italian Wedding Soup, 8oz.	180	6	1.5
Grilled Chicken Sandwich, no sides	410	12	2.5
Black Bean Veggie Burger, no sides	440	19	2.5
6oz. Sirloin, no sides	200	6	2.5
Baked Stuffed Chicken, no sides	360	14	7
Lemon Basil Salmon, no sides	490	34	4.5
Roasted Seasonal Vegetables, side	80	4.5	0
Steamed Seasonal Vegetables	100	7	1.5
Steamed Broccoli	70	6	1
Whole Grain Brown Rice, side *(Rice Pilaf is 40cal./1g. sat. fat more)*	180	6	.5

cont'd next page

WELL, YES AND NO

RESTAURANT UNO Chicago Grill YES!	Total Calories	Total Fat (g)	Saturated Fat (g)
Flatbread Crust Individual Pizza:			
BBQ Chicken 1/3	343	12	5
Cheese & Tomato, 1/3	326	15	7
Mediterranean, 1/3	306	15	5
Roasted Eggplant, Spinach & Feta, 1/3	293	11	3.5
Strawberry Smoothie	280	3.5	1.5
Mini Hot Chocolate Brownie Sundae	320	16	7
Mini All American Hot Apple Crumble	320	14	8
UNO Chicago Grill NO!			
UNO Breadstick, 1	160	8	2.5
Walnut Blueberry w/Goat cheese Salad	470	32	10
Fish and Chips	1200	81	12
Cheddar Burger w/Buffalo Cheddar	970	51	24
Mac & Cheese Deep Dish	1980	134	71
Farmers Market Indiv. Thick Crust Pizza, 1/3	526	35	8.5
Bread Pudding w/Caramel Sauce	900	54	33
Mini White Choc. Chunk Deep Dish Sundae	670	32	14
Mega Size Deep Dish Sundae *a good choice...for you and 26 friends!*	2700	130	76

CHINESE EXPRESS

Chinese food offers many lower fat items, but the sodium content in most of it is among the worst out there. So think about watching your sodium for a couple days afterwards, just to even things out.

TOP DOs AND DON'Ts

START with a clear soup like wonton, egg drop, or hot and sour to curb your appetite. But don't use the crispy noodles served with them; they're deep-fried.

PLAN to take half your food home. Servings are usually large for take-out and huge at nicer sit-down restaurants. You'll get two meals for the price of one.

STAY AWAY from combination plates, they usually have stir-fried rice and egg rolls which are laden with fat and calories.

AVOID "dipped in batter," "breaded," "twice-cooked" and of course, "deep-fried".

CREATE YOUR OWN PLATE

Order steamed instead of fried, especially deep-fried. Steamed vegetable dumplings or potstickers are a much better choice than egg rolls.

Since most items are made-to-order, tell them to:

- Leave out the MSG.
- Put the sauces on the side.
- Use very little oil in stir-fried dishes.
- Substitute chicken for pork or beef.
- Replace fried rice with steamed white rice. If they offer steamed brown rice, even better.
- Put in more vegetables.
- Go easy on the nuts or replace them with water chestnuts.

USE SOY SAUCE AS LITTLE AS POSSIBLE, AND ASK IF THEY HAVE THE "LIGHT" VERSION AVAILABLE–YOU'LL SAVE ON SODIUM.

ADD extra plain rice to other items– you'll lower the meal's overall fat, sodium, and calories.

WARNING: BROWN-COLORED FRIED RICE IS NOT THE SAME THING AS BROWN RICE. BROWN RICE IS WHOLE GRAIN RICE.

If you aren't already using chopsticks, try them. It can slow down your eating AND you'll get less sauce if you use them to get food from a platter instead of a spoon.

BEST CHOICES

- Chicken or beef with broccoli.

- Steamed or stir-fried vegetables, sometimes called vegetarian or Buddha's delight.

- Steamed or stir-fried fish, poultry, or tofu, topped with sweet-and-sour, plum, or duck sauce.

- Lo mein (light on oil) with vegetables, velvet chicken, yu-hsiang or moo shu chicken, and chop suey. All tend to have more vegetables.

WHAT LUCK! A fortune cookie only has about 25 calories. And that includes the fortune!

WORST CHOICES

FRIED FOODS like fried rice, egg rolls, spring rolls, fried wonton, crispy beef, egg foo yung, or battered items like General Tso's or Sweet and Sour Chicken. *One order of PF Chang's Double Pan-Fried Noodles with Chicken has 1030 cal., 48g fat, and 4790mg of sodium!!*

CONSIDER SUSHI

Yes, it's Japanese, but as popularity increases, many Chinese/Asian restaurants are adding it to their menus. While it can be a healthy choice, there are a few things to keep in mind:

• California, cucumber, asparagus, and other veggie rolls are great choices, just not the ones with cream cheese.

• Rolls with avocado have a bit more fat, but it's the good kind.

• Don't order deep-fried/tempura rolls.

• Know how many pieces per order, it makes a big difference in total calories and/or fat.

• One piece of tuna nigiri (raw fish over rice) usually has 40 calories, but a large piece can have 120.

• A 100 calorie seaweed salad can have 5 fat grams and 1,200 mg of sodium– get the cucumber salad!

• Miso soup can have up to 600 mg sodium for a one cup, 40 calorie serving.

Be alert to terms like crunchy (tempura bits), spicy (mayo-based sauce), and cream cheese– they add calories and fat. "Spicy" tuna rolls have __much__ more fat and calories than "plain".

WELL, YES AND NO

RESTAURANT Manchu Wok YES!	Total Calories	Total Fat (g)	Saturated Fat (g)
Spicy Chicken	150	9	1.5
Oriental Grilled Chicken	240	9	1.5
Green Bean Chicken	160	10	1.5
Beef & Broccoli	180	13	2.5
Kung Pao Chicken	180	12	2
Steamed Rice	370	0	0
Mixed Vegetables	130	10	1.5
Vegetable Egg Roll	150	6	1
Manchu Wok NO!			
Orange Chicken	400	21	3.5
Fried Rice	410	13	2.5
Lo Mein Noodles	300	17	3
Panda Express YES!			
"Wok Smart" items, per serving, *at or under*	250		
Mixed Vegetables, Side	70	.5	0
Steamed Rice	380	0	0
Black Pepper Chicken	200	10	2
Potato Chicken	190	9	1.5
Kung Pao Chicken	240	14	2.5
String Bean Chicken Breast	160	6	1
Grilled Teriyaki Chicken w/veggies	370	13.5	4
Broccoli Beef	120	4	.5
Shanghai Angus Steak	220	7	2
Veggie Spring Roll, 2	160	7	1

cont'd next page

WELL, YES AND NO

RESTAURANT **Panda Express YES!** (cont'd)	Total Calories	Total Fat (g)	Saturated Fat (g)
Chicken Potstickers, 3	220	11	2.5
Hot & Sour Soup	100	3.5	.5
Mandarin Sauce	160	0	0
Sweet & Sour Sauce	70	0	0
Panda Express NO!			
Beijing Beef	690	40	8
Orange Chicken	420	21	4
Chow Mein	490	22	4
Fried Rice	530	16	3
P.F. Chang's China Bistro YES! *(Gluten-Free versions have similar calories & fat.)* Chang's Chicken Lettuce Wraps, 1/4*	133	6	1.5
Chang's Vegetarian Lettuce Wraps, 1/4*	152	9	1
Vegetable Spring Rolls, 1	105	2.5	.5
Tuna Tataki	180	7	1
Pan-Fried Vegetable Dumplings, 1	60	2	0
Steamed Vegetable Dumplings, 1	40	0	0
Wonton Soup, cup	60	1	0
Hot & Sour Soup, cup	80	2.5	.5
Egg Drop Soup, cup	50	2	0
Spicy Tuna Roll	280	3	0
Orange Peel Beef, 1/3*	377	20	4
Mongolian Beef, 1/3*	240	13	3
Shaking Beef 1/3* *indicates serving portion of entire dish*	267	16	6

WELL, YES AND NO

RESTAURANT P.F. Chang's YES! (cont'd)	Total Calories	Total Fat (g)	Saturated Fat (g)
Beef w/Broccoli, 1/3*	290	12	3
Beef a La Sichuan, 1/3*	227	11	2.5
Pepper Steak, 1/3*	220	12	2.5
Chang's Spicy Chicken, 1/3*	273	12	2
Almond & Cashew Chicken, 1/3*	213	9	1.5
Moo Goo Gai Pan, 1/3*	140	5	1
Orange Peel Chicken, 1/3*	327	14	3
Sesame Chicken, 1/3*	297	12	2
Ginger Chicken w/Broccoli, 1/3*	153	4	.5
Cantonese-style Lemon Chicken 1/3*	250	12	2
Singapore Street Noodles, 1/3*	307	7	1
Beef Lo Mein, 1/3 entree*	240	7.5	1
Chicken Lo Mein, 1/3 entree*	237	6	1
Garlic Noodles, 1/4 entree*	180	4	1
Oolong Marinated Sea Bass, 1/2*	280	19	4.5
Hunan-style Hot Fish 1/2 *	325	16	2
Asian Grilled Salmon, 1/2*	305	17.5	2.5
Buddha's Feast Steamed, 1/2*	130	2	0
Buddha's Feast Stir-Fried, 1/2*	210	6	1
Shanghai Cucumbers, sml side, 1/2*	35	1.5	0
Edamame	400	17	2.5
Lo Mein Vegetable	490	6	.5
Spinach Stir-Fried w/Garlic, sml side, 1/2*	60	4	1
Spicy Green Beans, sml side, 1/2*	75	4	.5

cont'd next page

WELL, YES AND NO

RESTAURANT P.F. Chang's YES! (cont'd)	Total Calories	Total Fat (g)	Saturated Fat (g)
Sichuan-Style Asparagus, sml side, 1/2*	45	2	.5
White Rice Steamed, 6 oz.	300	1	0
Brown Rice Steamed, 6 oz.	310	1	0
Lunch Traditions, includes White Rice: *(with brown rice, 10-25cal. less and 1-2 more grams of total fat)*			
Beef w/Broccoli, 1/2*	335	9.5	2
Pepper Steak, 1/2*	340	11	2.5
Almond/Cashew Chicken, 1/2*	380	11	1.5
Sweet & Sour Chicken, 1/2*	355	9	1
Sesame Chicken, 1/2*	450	10	1.5
Asian Grilled Salmon, 1/2*	340	12	1.5
Ginger Chicken w/Broccoli, 1/2*	280	4	1
Chang's Spicy Chicken, 1/2*	395	11	1.5
Tiramisu, 1/2*	125	7	2
Chocolate Raspberry Wontons (1)	142	8	3
Sweet Vanilla Wontons (1)	132	11	4.5
P.F. Chang's NO!			
Crispy Green Beans, w/sauce, 1/2*	535	44	6
Shanghai Waldorf Salad w/chicken, 1/2*	330	24	4
Stir-Fried Eggplant, 1/2*	505	44	6
Coconut Curry Vegetables, 1/2*	525	39	12
Crispy Green Bean Sauce, 2oz.	310	33	4.5
The Great Wall of Chocolate, 1/2*	770	36	13
New York Style Cheesecake, 1/2*	450	29	18

A TASTE OF MEXICO

Is there really anything healthy at a Mexican restaurant? For the most part, they've earned their well-deserved reputation for serving high fat entrees–and then covering them with cheese! And as with most restaurants these days, the serving sizes at Mexican restaurants are simply huge. Surprisingly, with just a little bit of work you can actually eat well "south of the border." Some Mexican restaurants now feature "light" or "healthy" offerings that are almost always better than their regular menu items.

IT'S GOOD TO SHARE

Especially in Mexican restaurants. If you split an appetizer, an entree, and a dessert with a friend, on average, you'll each save around 1000 calories.

BEST CHOICES

Chicken or vegetable fajitas top the list—you actually get some vegetables. But be sure to ask that the tortillas NOT be brushed with oil.

- Black beans and plain white rice with a salad is a good, simple combination.

- Chicken, beef, and bean soft enchiladas, burritos or tamales.

- Chicken or beef soft taco, grilled fish tacos.

- Ceviche (citrus-marinated fish/seafood) is great when available. Limit chips if they're served with it.

- Grilled chicken or fish dishes.

- Mexican salads (called tostados), made with chicken or spicy beef are fine if you leave off the sour cream, guacamole, and fried tortilla shell or chips. Ask for extra veggies.

SPECIALTY SALADS can offer a great alternative to a high fat meal. Think about grilled/marinated chicken or fish, and add a little pico de gallo.

A LA CARTE SMART

ORDERING INDIVIDUAL items is really your best bet when eating Mexican. The special combination plates are usually loaded with too much food, fat, and calories.

COMBINE one or two items with a side salad or ask if you can replace higher fat items on a combo plate with a la carte offerings.

TELL YOUR WAITER NOT TO BRING THE BASKET OF CHIPS.

- *If they're there, you'll eat them.*
  When you consider that an average size basket of chips has between 640-1400 calories and 35-88 fat grams, it's plain to see the wisdom behind this idea. After all, who can *really* eat just one?

- *Can't swear them off entirely?*
  Place no more than 5 on a plate and ask for the rest to be taken away. And use only red salsa, stay away from the white style salsa or queso dips!

- *Skip the cheese nachos.*
  The average order has a *quarter pound* of cheese, 800 calories, and your entire allowance for saturated fat for the entire day.

WHAT'S ON TOP?

CHEESE: Adds a ton of calories and fat, and Mexican food is usually loaded with it inside and out. Eliminate as much as you can, where you can; including both shredded cheese and/or cheese-based sauces. Just ask if your food can be prepared without it.

SOUR CREAM: Best to forget it.

GUACAMOLE: High in fat, but the heart-healthy kind. And though it's packed with nutrition, go easy– just 1/4 cup adds a quick 100 or more calories.

HEALTHY OPTIONS: Salsa, ranchero sauce, pico de gallo, or red chile sauce deliver big flavor for little fat or calories. Use them as a substitute for less healthy choices or simply add them to your food for a bit of extra spice.

IF A RESTAURANT HAS BAKED TORTILLA CHIPS, REDUCED-FAT SOUR CREAM, WHOLE-WHEAT TORTILLAS, BROWN RICE, OR REDUCED FAT CHEESE AND/OR SALAD DRESSING TELL ALL YOUR FRIENDS ABOUT IT. (AND LET ME KNOW, TOO!)

BEANS AND RICE

REFRIED BEANS: Usually *loaded with fat*, and sometimes lard– leave them off your plate. Replace them with non-fried, cooked pinto or black beans, whether as a side dish, in or on entrées like burritos and tostados.

MEXICAN (SPANISH) RICE: Can be made with a little or a lot of oil and fat. Ask before ordering, or better yet, substitute plain rice and top with some pico de gallo.

WORST CHOICES

- Nachos Grande, are around 85 fat grams and 1400 calories (and 2700 mg sodium!)
- Taco Salad, not officially a "salad" with 70 or more fat grams!
- Beef Chimichangas can have 45 fat grams.

Remember, meat and cheese add unhealthy amounts of saturated fat to most items.

- Chimichangas, quesadillas, chile rellenos, fluatas and taquitos are all deep fried, adding too much fat and too many calories.
- Fried Ice Cream can have as much as 1100 calories and 60 grams of fat. Just say no!

WELL, YES AND NO

RESTAURANT	Total Calories	Total Fat (g)	Saturated Fat (g)
Chipotle Mexican Grill YES!			
Flour Tortilla (burrito), 1	300	10	1
Flour Tortilla (taco), 1	85	2.5	1
Crispy Taco Shell, 1	70	2.5	1
Barbacoa, 4oz.	165	7	2.5
Chicken, 4oz.	180	7	3
Steak, 4oz.	190	6.5	2
White Rice, 4oz.	185	4	0
Black or Pinto Beans, 4oz.	120	1	0
Fajita Vegetables, 2.5oz.	20	.5	0
Tomato Salsa, 3.5oz.	20	0	0
Corn Salsa, 3.5oz.	80	1.5	0
Red Tomatillo Salsa, 2oz.	25	1	0
Green Tomatillo Salsa, 2oz.	20	0	0
Guacamole, 3.5oz.	200	19	3
Chipotle Mexican Grill NO!			
Chips, 4oz.	570	27	3.5
Vinaigrette, 2oz.	215	15.5	2.5
El Pollo Loco YES!			
BRC Burrito	430	12	5
Grilled Chicken Tortilla Roll, no sauce	400	15	6
Chicken Breast, Skinless	180	3.5	1
Chopped Chicken Breast Meat	100	1.5	.5
The Original Pollo Bowl	610	10	2
Skinless Chick. Breast Meal, no tortilla strips	265	8	2

WELL, YES AND NO

RESTAURANT El Pollo Loco YES! (cont'd)	Total Calories	Total Fat(g)	Saturated Fat(g)
Crunchy Chicken Taco	300	17	5
Taco al Carbon	160	6	1.5
Grilled Chicken Salad, no dressing	240	8	2
Small Chicken Tortilla Soup w/strips	210	9	3
Chicken Tostado Salad, no dressing/shell	430	13	6
Mexican Cobb Salad, no dressing	520	25	7
Light Creamy Cilantro Dressing, 1 packet	70	5	1
Lowfat Citrus Vinaigerette	70	4	1
Double Chicken Wet Burrito	480	12	4
Skinny Quesadilla	460	17	8
Grilled Chicken & Kale Salad w/o dressing	420	24	4.5
Pinto Beans	200	4	.5
Rice	170	2.5	0
Mashed Potatoes w/Gravy add	110 10	1.5 0	.5 0
Fresh Vegetables, no margarine w/margarine add	35 25	0 3	0 0
Black Beans	200	3	.5
Corn Cobbette	160	5	1.5
Chicken Tortilla Soup, reg w/tortilla strips	210	9	3
6.5" Flour Tortilla, 2	220	7	2.5
6" Corn Tortilla, 2	110	1.5	0
Tortilla Chips	190	11	1.5
House Salsa, 1.5oz.	10	0	0

cont. next page

WELL, YES AND NO

RESTAURANT El Pollo Loco YES! (cont'd)	Total Calories	Total Fat (g)	Saturated Fat (g)
Pico de Gallo, 1.5oz.	15	1	0
Avocado Salsa, 1.5oz.	30	2.5	0
Churros, 2	300	18	4.5
Tres Leche Cake	230	15	6
El Pollo Loco NO!			
Ultimate Pollo Bowl	970	34	13
Chicken Tostado Salad in shell, no dressing	860	42	11
French Fries	330	17	2.5
Ranch Dressing, 1 pkt	230	24	3.5
Large Creamy Cilantro Dressing, 3 oz.	440	46	7
On The Border YES!			
Chicken Tortilla Soup, 1 cup	290	14	6
Citrus Chipotle Chicken Salad w/Mango Citrus Vinaigrette, as served	290	4	2
Chicken Salsa Fresca, as served	520	9	3
Jalapeno BBQ Salmon, as served	590	21	6
Chicken Enchiladas w/Sour Cream Sauce, as served	210	12	5
Ground Beef Enchiladas w/Chile con Carne as served	260	15	6
Achiote Chicken Tacos, w/rice	650	12	2
Best Lunch Chicken Fajitas, w/rice no tortillas, condiments, or beans	440	15	2
Chicken Flautas w/Chile con Queso, as served	370	26	8

WELL, YES AND NO

RESTAURANT On The Border YES! (cont'd)	Total Calories	Total Fat (g)	Saturated Fat (g)
Tostadas, Chicken, as served	130	5	2
On The Border NO!			
Grande Taco Salad w/Chicken, no dressing	1180	75	29
Classic Chimichanga, Ground Beef, no sauce, w/rice	1420	90	29
Dos XX Fish Tacos w/rice	1950	121	28
Rubio's Mexican Grill YES!			
*Tacos made with flour tortilla **add***	+50	+4	+2
*Burritos made with flour tortilla **add***	+20	+3	+1
*Burritos made with whole grain tortilla **subtract***	−20	−3	−1
Regal Springs Grilled Tilapia Taco	220	11	2
Chicken Street Taco	100	3	0
Classic Grilled Chicken Taco	240	13	4
HealthMex Grilled Chicken Burrito	550	11	3

Chopped Salad
   add Grilled Chicken
   add Grilled Mahi Mahi
	340
	100
	110
		18
		1
		2
			5
			0
			0

Chopped Chicken Salad	440	19	5
Chicken Enchilada 1, w/beans & rice	385	15	6
Original Fish Taco	310	20	2
Fish Taco Especial	370	25	4
Grilled Atlantic Salmon Taco	230	10	2
Blackened Mahi Mahi Taco	220	10	2
Classic Grilled Steak Taco	200	8	3
Steak Street Taco	90	4	1

cont. next page

WELL, YES AND NO

RESTAURANT Rubio's Mexican Grill YES! (cont'd)	Total Calories	Total Fat (g)	Saturated Fat (g)
Rubio's Street Tacos w/steak (3)	360	12	3
Citrus Rice, reg	150	2	0
Balsamic & Roasted Veggie Salad	200	10	1
Chicken Tortilla Soup, a la carte	240	7	2
Light Balsamic Vinaigrette, 2oz.	100	6	0
Mexican Rice, reg	140	2	0
Pinto Beans, lrg	370	3	1
Black Beans, reg.	130	2	1
Salsa Picante	20	1	0
Key Lime Cake Pop	150	8	4
Churro, 1	160	9	5
Rubio's Mexican Grill NO!			
Grilled Gourmet Steak Taco	300	20	7
Grilled Gourmet Chicken Taco	320	19	7
Grilled Ono Burrito	700	31	7
Beer Battered Fish Burrito	850	53	10
Grilled Veggie Burrito	750	40	12
Steak Quesadilla	1230	75	32
Cheese Quesadilla	970	50	24
Cheese Enchiladas, Fire-Roasted Sauce, 2	800	38	17
Nachos Grande Chicken	1390	80	28
Chipotle Ranch Dressing, 2oz.	260	26	4
Taco Bell (see Fast Food)			

THAT'S ITALIAN

Good news! Italian food provides a lot of choices, making it one of your best bets for dining out. Knowing a few basics will allow you to enjoy your meal without worrying about your waistline. But with lots of entrees high in cheese and high fat meats, you'll need to proceed with caution.

GOOD BEGINNINGS

ALWAYS BEGIN with a healthy soup or salad to help you feel full; minestrone, gazpacho, and escarole are all good choices for soup.

TRY AN APPETIZER of marinated vegetables, but avoid antipastos; they're loaded with cheeses and cured meats.

GARLIC BREAD is about five times higher in fat than plain white bread. Plain bread dipped in a little olive oil is a great alternative.

BEST CHOICES

Ordering entrées that are mostly pasta, avoiding dishes with lots of cheese like lasagna and manicotti, and choosing items that are broiled, baked or grilled instead of breaded or sautéed are all great ideas.

• Cheese ravioli with tomato or marinara sauce. It's usually about half the calories of an order of spaghetti and meatballs.

• Chicken piccata, cacciatore, pollo alla verdicchio.

• Fish broiled in lemon sauce.

• Meatballs with marinara, not meat sauce.

QUICK TIP: ASK FOR THE CHEESE TO BE LEFT OFF THE TOP OF YOUR ENTRÉE. USE A LITTLE PARMESAN INSTEAD AND SAVE LOTS OF FAT AND CALORIES!

• Pasta with marinara sauce, pasta primavera, linguine with red sauce

• Primavera. Lots of vegetables usually make this a good choice. Be sure to tell the waiter which sauce you want with it.

• Veal piccata, cacciatore, and francese.

For desert try Italian ice rather than tortoni, cannoli, or spumoni. Look for sorbets and "mini" desserts when available. A biscotti with coffee is a nice way to end a meal.

KNOW YOUR SAUCES

Be sure to order ALL sauces on the side. You'll eat less than they would serve.

- Tomato, marinara, and vegetable sauces are always the best choices.

For dishes that are mostly pasta, these are ok:

- Bolognese and meat sauce have more fat and calories but are still reasonable choices.

- Red or white clam sauce is fine, but be sure the white clam sauce doesn't include cream.

- White wine sauce is ok.

- Lemon butter sauce (sometimes called piccata) is usually a pretty good choice, but can be swimming in butter. Ask how it's prepared before you order.

- Pesto sauce is uncooked with olive oil, basil, garlic, pine nuts, and Parmesan cheese. It's still high in calories but doesn't have the bad saturated fat of cream sauces.

These should always be avoided:

- Alfredo, carbonara, and cream or cheese based sauces!

When having pizza order double veggies, light cheese. Leave off the anchovies, sausage, and pepperoni. Go for thin crust and only eat one or two pieces; then bring the rest home or back to work. Some places have huge slices, so keep that in mind.

WORST CHOICES

- Fettuccine Alfredo, linguine with cream sauce, meat lasagna, meat with cheese cannelloni, and veal parmigiana.

Remember, "Parmigiana" means that it's dipped in milk and egg, breaded, sautéed in oil or butter, and comes with marinara sauce and melted cheese.

Some good examples of the worst:

- Eggplant Parmesan usually has over 1000 calories and about 100 grams of fat.
- Fettuccine Alfredo weighs in at about 700 calories and 40 fat grams.

When at Olive Garden™: eat lots of unlimited salad/ soup. Get low fat dressing on the side, the bread sticks plain and order from the "Lighter Italian Fare" menu.

WELL, YES AND NO

RESTAURANT CiCi's Pizza YES!	Total Calories	Total Fat (g)	Saturated Fat (g)
1 slice = 1/10 of 12" buffet pizza, which is smaller slices than their take-out or other pizza places.			
Mac & Cheese Pizza, 1 slice	190	4.5	2
Ole Pizza, 1 slice	180	6	2.5
Pepperoni Pizza, 1 slice	190	8	4
Spinach Alfredo, 1 slice	150	5	2.5
Zesty Veggie Pizza, 1 slice	170	5	2
Buffalo Chicken Pizza, 1 slice	160	5	2
Bavarian Dessert, 1 slice	130	3	.5
CiCi's Pizza NO!			
Pepperoni and Beef Pizza	230	11	5
Pepperoni and Sausage Pizza	220	10	4.5
Dominos YES!			
1 slice = 1/8 of 12" (med) or 14" (lrg) Hand-Tossed Cheese Pizza, med, 1 slice	211	8	4
Hand-Tossed Cheese Pizza, lrg, 1 slice	290	11	5
Thin Crust Cheese Pizza, lrg, 1 slice	226	12	
Veggies Pizza, lrg, 1 slice	270	10	4
Grilled Chicken & Veggies Pizza, lrg, 1 slice	280	9	4
Fire, Hot or Mild Chicken Wings, 4	200	13	3.5
Boneless Chicken, 3 pieces	150	6	1
Grilled Chicken Caesar Salad, 1/2 bowl	85	3.5	1.5
Lite Italian Dressing	20	1	0
Cinna Stix, 1	117	6	1

If you must have meat on your pizza, keep it to one.

cont'd next page

WELL, YES AND NO

RESTAURANT Dominos NO!	Total Calories	Total Fat (g)	Saturated Fat (g)
Buffalo Chicken Oven Baked Sandwich	830	41	16
Cinna Stix, no icing, 4pc	470	25	4.5
Chicken Bacon Ranch Sandwich	870	45	16
Chicken Alfredo, in tin	600	29	16
Pasta Primavera, in tin	540	27	16
Fazoli's YES!			
"400 Calories Or Less" menu items			
Breadstick, dry, 1	100	2	0
Baked Spaghetti	570	20	12
Kids Meal, Fettuccine Alfredo	310	11	4.5
Spaghetti or Penne w/Marinara Sauce, reg	610	7	0
w/Meatballs, *add*	250	18	8
Ravioli w/Marinara Sauce	450	14	8
Grilled Chicken, topping	110	2.5	0
Cheese Pizza, 1 slice	310	14	7
Lite Baked Spaghetti	330	10	6
Cherry Apple Almond Salad, no dressing	370	14	4
Italian Lemon Ice w/Strawberry, lrg	270	0	0
Fazoli's NO!			
Chicken Broccoli Penne	870	42	19
Penne w/Creamy Basil Chicken	870	42	19
Baked Spaghetti w/Meatballs	820	38	20
Spaghetti or Penne w/Meat Sauce, reg	720	16	3.5
Fazoli's Original Submarino	790	37	14

WELL, YES AND NO

RESTAURANT	Total Calories	Total Fat (g)	Saturated Fat (g)
Fazoli's NO! (cont'd)			
Ranch Dressing, 1.5oz.	220	24	4
NY Style Cheesecake w/Strawberry Topping	630	45	26
Olive Garden YES!			
Breadstick (w/garlic-butter spread)	140	2.5	.5
Bruschetta, whole appetizer	680	22	6
Garden-Fresh Salad, 1 serving, no dressing (get *Lite Italian or Parmesan-Peppercorn on the side*)	60	2	0
Minestrone Soup, 1 serving	110	1.5	0
Pasta e Fagioli Soup, 1 serving	180	6	2.5
Zuppa Toscana Soup, 1 serving	220	15	6
Chicken & Gnocchi Soup, 1 serving	250	14	5
You can always order a lunch portion, even in the evening. (items don't include bread/sides)			
Garlic Rosemary Chicken, lunch size	400	16	6
better than dinner size which has	540	20	7
Cheese Ravioli w/Marinara, lunch size	570	23	11
Cheese Ravioli w/Marinara, dinner size	740	29	13
Chicken Parmigiana, lunch size	620	27	7
Spaghetti w/Meat Sauce, lunch size	460	16	6
Spaghetti w/Chicken Meatballs, lunch size	670	22	8
Chicken Parmigiana Sandwich, half	430	16	3.5
Chicken Abruzzi	540	17	6
Grilled Chicken Toscano	760	28	12
Herb-Grilled Salmon	470	23	5
Dolcini-size Desserts, 1 pc *all at or under*	290	21	10

cont'd next page

WELL, YES AND NO

RESTAURANT	Total Calories	Total Fat (g)	Saturated Fat (g)
Olive Garden NO!			
Calamari, whole appetizer	680	44	4.5
Grilled Chicken Caesar Salad	670	45	9
Fettuccine Alfredo, lunch size	700	45	27
Chicken Alfredo, dinner size	1540	97	56
Spaghetti & Meatballs, lunch size	740	35	13
Chicken Parmigiana, dinner size	1010	49	13
Lasagna Classico, dinner size	960	58	31
Chicken Scampi	1310	76	29
White Chocolate Raspberry Cheesecake	890	62	36
Pizza Hut YES!			
Note: 1 slice pizza= 1/8 of med-12" or lrg-14"			
Hand-Tossed Cheese Pizza, med, 1 slice	210	8	4
Hand-Tossed Cheese Pizza, lrg, 1 slice	290	11	6
Thin 'N Crispy Cheese Pizza, med, 1 slice	190	8	4
Thin 'N Crispy Cheese Pizza, lrg, 1 slice	260	11	6
Thin 'N Crispy Pepperoni Pizza, med, 1 slice	210	10	5
Veggie Lovers Hand-Tossed Pizza, lrg, 1 slice	260	9	4
Veggie Lovers Thin 'N Crispy Pizza, lrg, 1 slice	240	9	4
Veggie Lovers 6" Personal Pan Pizza	550	20	8
Buffalo Traditional Bone-In Chicken Wings, 2	130	7	1.5
Cinnamon Sticks, 2	160	4.5	.5
Pizza Hut NO!			
BBQ Lovers 6" Personal Pan Pizza	740	36	14
Meat Lover's Large Pan Pizza, 1 slice	460	27	9

WELL, YES AND NO

RESTAURANT	Total Calories	Total Fat (g)	Saturated Fat (g)
Pizza Hut NO! (cont'd)			
Supreme Stuffed Crust Pizza, lrg, 1 slice	360	18	8
Garlic Parmesan Crispy Bone-In Wings, 2	290	23	4.5
Ranch Dipping Sauce, 1.5oz.	220	23	3.5
Romano's Macaroni Grill YES!			

CAUTION! Romano's Macaroni Grill no longer publishes its total fat gram information. Saturated fat is listed, but total fat will always be higher. Very often, MUCH higher!

	Total Calories	Total Fat (g)	Saturated Fat (g)
Goat Cheese Peppadew Peppers, appetizer	350	n/a	6
Minestrone Soup	160	n/a	0
Pomodorina Soup, bowl	170	n/a	3
Caesar Salad, w/dressing (side)	240	n/a	5
Mediterranean Orzo Salad	610	n/a	7
Fettuccine Gorgonzola (lunch)	320	n/a	17
Caprese Sandwich	630	n/a	10
Spaghetti Bolognese	630	n/a	7
Italian Sausage & Potatoes	520	n/a	5
Pollo Caprese	720	n/a	11
Brick-Oven Olives	280	n/a	5
Romano's Macaroni Grill NO!			
Baked Mozzarella Fonduta	1160	n/a	37
Classic Italian Bake	1480	n/a	38
Ricotta Meatballs & Spaghetti w/bolognese	1130	n/a	22
Chicken Scaloppine	1110	n/a	37
Parmesan-Crusted Sole	1330	n/a	41
Mama's Trio	2040	n/a	52

RESTAURANT INDEX

CUSTOMIZE
Wealthy, Healthy & Wise
WITH YOUR MESSAGE

- **INTRODUCTORY LETTER OR GREETING:** The first two pages in this book are available for your company's personalized message.

- **PRODUCT OR SERVICE PROMOTION:** You can also highlight your company's offerings on the inside back cover. It's a great opportunity to further your marketing efforts for new or existing product lines and services.

- **FRONT COVER BRANDING:** For larger quantity orders, we can add your company name or logo.

**Contact Gilbert Press
at
1-314-838-5942**